Stories of the CLANS

For Maurice Fleming
and the staff of

"The Scots Magazine"

who do so much
for Scotland

"Better a swift death on the battlefield
than a lingering one in bed"

Gaelic Proverb

Published by Lang Syne Publishers Ltd
45 Finnieston St., Glasgow
Tel: 041-204 3104
Printed by Dave Barr Print
45 Finnieston Street, Glasgow
Tel: 041-221 2598

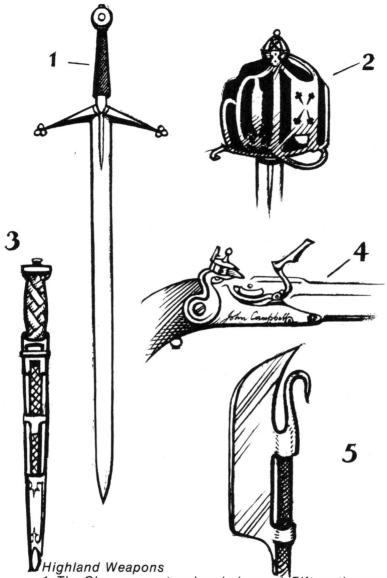

Highland Weapons
1. The Claymore or two-handed sword (Fifteenth or early Sixteenth century)
2. Basket hilt of Broadsword made in Stirling, 1716
3. Highland Dirk — Eighteenth century
4. Steel Pistol (detail) made in Doune
5. Head of Lochaber Axe as carried in the '45 and earlier.

PREFACE

In the following pages Rennie McOwan, a distinguished son of Scotland, explores the clan system and its origins. The different tartans, mottoes, territories and sept names are presented clearly and concisely.

Stirring stories of the clans are told and many fascinating points emerge.

The Gordon, Earl of Huntly, showed great courage on the sacffold, saying:-"You may take my head from my shoulders but not my heart from my sovereign".

Clansmen had many strange beliefs. New born-babies were dipped in winter rivers so that the icy waters would toughen them for later life.

One leader was said to be immune to bullets and rode a black horse which had been gifted by the Devil.

The Chisholm Clan had a chanter known as "The Maiden of the Sandal" which was credited with super-natural powers.

On Skye there is a flag at Dunvegan Castle which is capable of magical things but which must never be waved for a fourth time otherwise it will be useless.

Stories behind the coats of arms belonging to different clans are also explored. There is a marvellous example of survival against all odds in the axe, laurel and cypress which make up the MacLean arms. Equally interesting is the background to the stag's head which graces the MacKenzie family's armorial bearings.

The author tells of the clan which was forbidden weapons, had their name hated, womenfolk branded, and children removed to other areas where they were reared by rival clansmen.

Find out too about Alastair MacGregor and 11 of his chieftains who were hanged at the Mercat Cross in Edinburgh, the link between Clan Grant and the mighty Canadian Pacific Railway, the reason why many MacKay babies were given the Christian name of Gustavus, how an ancestor of the Fergussons gave Scotland our national flag, the incredible luck of Cameron of Lochiel, the horror of the battle known as "The Field of the Shirts", the Robertson who fought in three Jacobite risings spanning 57 years, and the chief who tricked his Viking enemies into believing he had three armies at his immediate command ...

Traditions & Roles of the Clans

THE word Clan has an international fascination and is recognised in many countries as meaning a grouping of people held together by a special bond.

It has been used for a special in-group of Hollywood film stars, and for Mafia-type families or firms. Fortunately, there is no direct Clan connection in the Ku Klux Klan, the secret organisation born in the southern states in a bid to protect the defeated Southerners in the American Civil War from carpet-baggers, exploitation or harassment and which degenerated into an anti-Negro 'hate' organisation. The name is a corruption of *Kuklos*, the Greek for a circle.

But its origin is firmly Scottish. The Gaelic word *Clann* means Children and typifies the special, close relationship that once existed between a Chief and his people.

In discussing this relationship it is essential to distinguish between different centuries and periods. Some chiefs betrayed their people and vice versa and others showed the most impressive two-way loyalty in the face of persecution and powerful enemies.

Broadly speaking, when the old Celtic laws operated, the bond between Chief and Clansmen and women was very close. It was only when feudal ideas were incorporated into Scotland that a gulf gradually developed and an atmosphere of 'private landlord' and subservient tenant eventually replaced the all-for-one-and-one-for-all relationship, a decline that eventually led to the despotic behaviour of some Clan 'chiefs', by now anglicised landlords and class-conscious, who evicted their people from their ancestral lands during the 19th Century Clearances so that they could make money from rearing sheep on the cleared land. This led to mass emigration.

The near-desert appearance of much of the Highlands dates mainly from this time.

Hillwalkers and mountaineers who believe they have a moral right to go, unhindered, to Scotland's mountains, glens and moors (while, rightly, respecting deer-stalking dates and other estate needs) are sometimes ridiculed if they claim a kinship with the people of past centuries who, together, owned Highland land.

But they have factual history to support this point of view.

Under ancient Celtic rule and custom land belonged to the clan, not to a person. The chief held a superiority of it, but only in name of the clan, as its 'father'.

As mountaineer and writer W.H.Murray points out in his definitive book, "Rob Roy MacGregor - His Life and Times" (Richard Drew, Glasgow) the chief in all clans represented their common ancestry, his office being hereditary not to his person but to his ruling family, from whom successors were elected.

The early clan system, therefore, was aristocratic but not feudal. The people were free and could speak as equals to their chief, as children to father. This changed in later centuries but even as late as the 19th century and the time of the Napoleonic wars it is recorded that regular British Army officers looked askance at the Glengarry chief cracking jokes in Gaelic with his men on parade, a cordial bond and relationship which was foreign to the harsher and more class-conscious Army structures of the day.

Some Clans were large and could put thousands of men under arms, others were small and could only provide a handful.

Some major Clans or families lost their lands by being on the losing side of Scottish power-struggles -"broken men", in the popular phrase - and were absorbed by others for all time. Some Clansmen, as with the MacGregors when they were persecuted by Scottish monarchs and their very name was banned, temporarily took other names.

Again, in examining the size of a Clan, or its ancestral area, it is necessary to draw a distinction between different centuries.

Major features were, of course, common to all. Highland Clans were Gaelic speaking, a rich, beautiful and sensitive language which is one of the oldest in Europe and which still survives in the Western Isles and some mainland pockets. In modern times there has been an immense upsurge of interest in the language on the part of non-Gaelic speaking Scots, many from Highland stock, who are endeavouring to learn the language. The music of the Gaelic people is still vibrant and each year local festivals, and a mammoth national festival, called Mods, are held.

The fact that the Highlands were Gaelic speaking and the Lowlands Scots or Scots/English (although Galloway, in south-west Scotland was once a Gaelic speaking area) helped draw a psychological boundary line which made many southerners regard Highland areas as foreign land.

In recent times Border families have been listed as Clans (and some, indeed, once owned northern territory) and have adapted a family tartan but, strictly speaking, they are not Clans and this book mainly confines itself to north of the Highland line.

So language was a bond among Clans and a barrier to others. In the 1715 Jacobite Rising the commander of the Hanoverian King George I's forces in Scotland, the Duke of Argyll, known to his fellow Highlanders as Red-John-of-the-Battles, ordered his men at the Battle of Sheriffmuir in 1715 not to press home their advantage on the the Clansmen who fought on the opposing, Jacobite, side. "Spare the blue bonnets", he said. It was a recognition of their common background and culture. There were exceptions to this, of course, because there were also some ferocious feuds and massacres.

Another barrier was geography - the Grampian mountains are like a wall stretching close to the narrow waist of Scotland, and north of it lay the Clan lands.

The town of Stirling is said to be a buckle that clasps Highlands and Lowlands together and author Neil Munro in his splendid historical novel, "The New Road", wrote:"The Grampians, like ramparts, stood between two ages, one of paper, one of steel: on either side were peoples foreign to each other. Since roads had been in Scotland they had reached to Stirling, but at Stirling they had stopped, and on the castle rock the sentinel at nightfall saw the mists go down upon a distant land of bens and glens on which a cannon or a carriage wheel had never yet intruded".

The probing Romans never managed to subdue the Highlands, the Clans were prominent in the successful Scottish Wars of Independence against the invading armies of Edward I and II of England, they resisted General Monk, Cromwell's hatchetman in Scotland, but eventually the military roads built in the

18th century by General Wade and his subordinate, Major Caulfeild, the Hanoverian forts built at strategic sites in the Highlands and the brutal clamp-down by the Hanoverian government after the 1745 Jacobite Rising failed, spelled the beginning of the end for the way of life of the Clans.

The power of the chiefs was broken, tartan was banned as were weapons and the pipes, the Clan system was broken up and all that is left now are memories, modern clan societies, and thousands of Scots, or people of Scots descent, who have a pride in an ancestry that was staunch, courageous, colourful, war-like. cultured. vigorous and full of zest.

Myths and the secret of MacFarlane's Lantern

It is commonly said that the Highlander of old was barbarous, mailny because he was ferocious in battle, but poetry, song and music flourished in what were cruel ages. Many people could not read or write but it would be wrong to call them illiterate because there was a strong oral tradition of saga and music. Chiefs' sons were frequently educated abroad, many could speak French as well as Gaelic and English, and learning was respected. Rob Roy MacGregor's house contained several books and he had relatives who were on the lecturing staff of universities.

The people were *not* crofters = crofting (broadly speaking, small 'farms' or holdings) is a 19th century creation following the clearing of people from their ancestral lands and when the large deer-stalking and sporting estates superseded, or were created alongside sheep farms.

The Highlands of old operated a cattle economy; thousands of small, black cattle were reared. Goats were also commonly kept. Fishing and deer-hunting were also carried out.

The word black-mail originates from the Trossachs area in the Southern Highlands. It is not so bad as it sounds. The MacGregors and others said to Lowland landowners 'pay us money and we won't steal your cattle and we won't let anyone else do that either'. It was a kind of primitive policing. Blackmail derives from black for the colour of the cattle (the present-day shaggy Highland cattle are a 19th century crossbreed) and mail from an old Scots word for rent.

8

In the late 18th century and the 19th century large cattle droves went from the Highlands to the great fairs at Crieff and Falkirk, many of them bought by Lowland or English dealers, and some went further south to markets near Carlisle and Norwich, the roast beef of old England going south from Scotland.

Scots who migrated, or were forcibly transported, to what is now the United States, sometimes did spectularly well in the cattle business and some, or their descendants, left their Clan mark on the map forever, as with the old Chisholm trail.

Earlier, it was recognised that cattle-reiving (stealing) was a manly pursuit and many became expert at 'borrowing' cattle from their neighbours or protecting their own. It was said of the MacFarlanes, who lived on Loch Lomond-side, that they "paid their daughters' tochers by the light of the Michelmas moon" = i.e. they got the cash for their daughters' dowries by stealing someone else's cattle and did it in the autumn when there was enough darkness for concealment and enough moonlight to see what they were doing. The moon was known as MacFarlane's Lantern.

All this fitted the Highlander for war, long marches, concealment, toughness, ambushes, sleeping in the open, organisation and discipline. It is sometimes said of Highland armies that they were unreliable, that they deserted but such charges need to be seen against the need to temporarily return home for harvests and sowing, they were good judges of when enough was enough, although they were also capable of reckless courage, and the so-called wild Highland charge was, in fact, a controlled affair of great power, and calling for discipline and good timing. They were in great demand by European monarchs as mercenaries.

Of course, there were unsavoury incidents, the breaking of hospitality at the Glen Coe Massacre in 1692, the MacGregors placing the head of the King's forester in Glen Artney on the table at Ardvorlich Castle for his daughter to find, the MacDonalds on Eigg being suffocated or burned to death in a cave by the MacLeods, and many others, or individual acts of bravado like the youthful Colkitto MacDonald, who was to become the military genius behind the Marquis of Montrose's bid to win Scotland for Charles I in 1645/6, eating a live toad in front of his boyhood friends to show how tough he was.

Highland babies were dipped in winter-rivers not long after birth to toughen them, and old Cameron of Lochiel once kicked a pillow made of snow and covered in a plaid from below his son's head and accused him of being soft.

But there was plenty of chivalry as well. One example must suffice. One day a band of MacDonalds, including one Iain MacAllein, raided the Grant lands in Strathspey and were surrounded by 60 men. Iain MacAllein offered his sword in surrender and as the Laird of Grant's son stepped forward to take it he spun the weapon and cut the Grant down.

The MacDonalds got away but on the way home to Glen Coe Iain MacAllein was overcome with remorse and turned back. He found the wounded man and went to get water for him from the burn. When he returned young Grant shot him with a pistol, breaking his thigh-bone. They then lay in their blood watching one another.

Iain MacAllein pushed himself up on one knee and suggested they continue the fight. Grant agreed but when he saw Iain MacAllein could only kneel and he, with difficulty, could stand he proposed friendship instead. They agreed and later when Grant Clansmen arrived, they were both carried to Strathspey where Iain MacAllein stayed for a year. Both young men recovered and remained good friends.

Times could be hard in past centuries and sometimes after hard winters and poor springs starvation could threaten but the open air and pastoral way of life in an 18th century Highland glen was immeasurably healthier than, say, 19th century life in a Glasgow slum or a Lanarkshire coal pit.

The Gaelic pattern of the shieling, when each spring and summer the people took themselves from the loch shores and the lower glens and straths up into the upper glens and moors, was a time of gaiety and festivity. There the people lived in makeshift huts and supervised the grazing of their cattle and goats, fattening them for sale or for the winter and making butter and cheese.

Many held their land by the sword and distrusted -often to their disadvantage - charters and papers prepared in far-off Stirling or Edinburgh by Kings and scheming nobles.

Like the North American Indians, they lived at harmony with the landscape and with wild things. It is 20th century man with his pollution and 'development' that is the wrecker of beauty and is the true barbarian.

They considered war a manly pursuit, and with only oatmeal to sustain them could march for miles and then fight a battle at the end of it. They fought common enemies and one another and as late as the 18th century rocked the British Government to its heels in the 1745 Jacobite Rising, and their successors fought bravely in Britain's colonial wars and in modern times.

Their weapons were broadsword and claymore (literally, big or great sword), bows and arrows, Lochaber axes, dirks (a long dagger) and targe (a round shield) and, in later centuries, muskets and pistols.

Led well, there has possibly been no finer infantry. They were uneasy in street fighting or facing cannon and musket-fire, but in a charge - as Neil Munro says -they would carry the very Gates of Hell even if the Devil himself stood in the portals.

It is entirely fitting that the statue on the tall column-monument at Glenfinnan, in the West Highlands, which marks where Prince Charles Edward Stuart raised his Standard in 1745 in the last bid to win the throne of Britain for the Stuarts, depicts not the Prince, as is commonly thought, but an ordinary Clansman.

Despite huge rewards being offered, persecution and hardship, no one betrayed the Prince when he was a fugitive.

When the Jacobite chiefs fled overseas their people often paid two rents, one to the Hanoverian landlord and one, secretly, to their chief.

The story of the Clans is both gory and glorious, of plotting and power struggles, of cruelties and generosity, of fierce loyalties and great passions, of love of one's native place, of tenacity and perseverance, of martial behaviour and dress.

It is not surprising that people feel a bond of sympathy, as well as blood, with such a race. The search for 'roots' is a modern phenomenon, perhaps born from the insecurity of 20th century man, and for many the search will find an honoured resting place in the Highlands of Scotland.

"*People feel a bond of sympathy, as well as blood, with such a race ...*"

12

All you need to know about Tartan

TARTAN has an immense fascination for people, the colours, the patterns, the uniqueness, the style and the associations with martial deeds and great events.

The transatlantic custom of the Kirking-of-the-Tartan, when tartan is taken by the Clan societies to church and reverently blessed, has no firm historical links with Scottish practice, but it is a legitimate expression of the cloth's special place in Scottish hearts and the part it has played in Highland and Scottish history.

General Sir Colin Campbell, at the Relief of Lucknow in 1857 during the Indian Mutiny, was exasperated by delays and shouted: "Bring forrit (forward) the tartan, let my own lads at them!"

He was addressing Colonel Ewart, of the 93rd Highlanders (the "Thin Red Line" of Balaclava fame) whose men were on a ridge behind him.

They had marched through the night to battle with thousands of mutinous sepoys who had massacred many European men, women and children and who were now halting Colin Campbell's brave Punjabi troops as they tried to fight their way through a breach in a wall.

A piper played "On With the Tartan" as the breach was stormed and six Victoria Crosses were won.

Dr. Micheil MacDonald, director of the Scottish Tartans Society, points out that the word tartan here was used as a kind of shorthand to personify the martial virtues of the Highlander.

(The Society operate the Scottish Tartans Museum in Comrie, Perthshire, and are rightly regarded as the definitive authority on tartan matters. Their motto is "Bring forrit the tartan").

The link between bravery in the past and bravery in modern times is well shown by a McBean Clansman at Culloden in 1746 who felled over a dozen Hanoverians before being cut down himself and Commander Alan L.Bean, the U.S. astronaut, conscious of his Highland links, who took MacBean tartan with him to the moon and later donated a fragment to the Comrie Museum.

There are widespread misconceptions about tartan. In past centuries people did not wear red-and-green tartans in one glen and blue-and-yellow in the next.

The modern Clan tartan patterns were formalised in recent centuries and some are derived from romantic 19th century writings which owe more to imagination than research, but their precise styles and colours have now received a formal recognition in their own right. At the same time, in the 18th and 19th centuries, Chiefs and other experts did try and identify the patterns worn in earlier years.

Nevertheless, it must be stressed that modern Highland dress is directly based on Highland dress of the past, that people living in one area could, and did recognise people from another area by the way their apparel had been woven, and that tartan has an ancient pedigree.

In the period before individual tartan-designs developed, Clansmen during war situations wore plant badges in their bonnets to identify one another, bog myrtle for the Campbells, ivy for the Gordons, yew for the Frasers, crowberry for the MacLeans, juniper for the Ross's, oak or thistle for the Stewarts, pine for the MacGregors and so on.

The standard definition of tartan, *breacan* as the Gaelic has it, is " a kind of woollen cloth woven in stripes of various colours at right angles so as to form a regular pattern", but the sett, the design and pattern is strictly formalised and very precise.

Vegetable dyes used in the past were often extremely lovely and 'soft' and can now be expertly matched by modern chemical dyes which also produce bright and more strident colours.

14

It is not possible here for space reasons to give a detailed history but three events helped preserve tartan in the years following its proscription by the Hanoverian Government after the 1745 Jacobite Rising failed. When the ban was lifted some Clan chiefs did make efforts some years later to restore or re-call the dress of their forefathers. Most Clan Societies were formed in the 19th century and later, and they, too, gave prominence to Highland dress which in our own day has come to be regarded as the national dress for the whole of Scotland. Sir Walter Scott's romanticism and Queen Victoria's 'Balmorality' have both been criticised for portraying the Highlander as if he lived in a tartan Never-Never land but, nevertheless, it all helped create an admiring and sympathetic climate of opinion. Finally the raising of Highland regiments during the Napoleonic Wars and the imperial wars gave the kilt and tartan its old military place once again.

My own father, who fought with the Queen's Own Cameron Highlanders during the First World War, wore the kilt in action and kept it until his death many years later.

Our own town pipe band in Stirling nowadays wear a tartan specially created by the firm of William Wilson & Son, of Bannockburn, who in the 19th century were major manufacturers of tartan for the Army and who are now defunct.

Highlanders long ago wore a long plaid, 12 to 18 feet long and nearly five feet wide. A belt was laid down, the plaid was folded lengthwise on top making several pleats at the near-end. The wearer would lie on top, buckle the belt and so rise kilted. The long end was drawn loosely up the back and either wound round both shoulders for warmth or over the left shoulder and across the chest, then round the back again to finish over the same shoulder where it would be pinned. The loops were left to hang at each hip and the sword arm was left free.

The natural wool and its warmth made it a superb garment for campaigning. It was often discarded in battle and men fought in their shirts, sometimes with the tails knotted between their legs.

A little tartan kilt, (the philabeg), minus the rest of the plaid, evolved and the modern kilt is derived from that although pipe bands members, office-bearers of

Highland societies and some others still wear a modern version of the whole plaid.

Highland dress nowadays tends to be a matter of dress-wear, dances, parties, Highland games, formal functions, dinners, rather than everyday wear (although there are exceptions to this), and its main components are stylised versions of functional garments of past times.

For example, kilt and plaid pins and brooches have become highly ornamental (it is true, of course, that some in the past were also richly made), so has the once fuctional sporran or pouch. The sgian dubh, or black knife, worn in the stocking, was once a skinning or eating knife but it is purely symbolic nowadays. The black 'holes' punched in the leather-design of modern brogues (shoes) recall the days when deer-skin brogues had holes to let the water run out when Highlanders waded burns and rivers or crossed wet ground.

But the dress today is still striking and manly and full-dress wear can be magnificent. The kilt should be worn with dignity, and never guyed up.

A very helpful guide to wearing the kilt is J.Charles Thompson's "So You're Going to Wear the Kilt", published by Paul Harris, Edinburgh.

Visitors to Scotland are sometimes unaware that tartan was once banned.

The Government were so shaken by the Jacobite Risings that on August 1, 1747, they set out to end Highland dress.

The proclamation said..."no man or boy within that part of Great Britain called Scotland other than such as shall be employed as officers and soldiers in his Majesty's Forces, shall, on any pretext whatever, wear or put on the clothes, commonly called Highland clothes (that is to say) the plaid, philabeg, or little Kilt, trewse, shoulder-belts, or any part whatever of what peculiarly belongs to the Highland garb: and that no tartan or party-coloured plaid or stuff shall be used for great coats or upper coats, and if any such person shall presume after the first said day of August to wear or put on the aforesaid garments or any part of them, every such person so offending...shall be liable to be transported to any of his Majesty's plantations beyond the seas, there to remain for the space of seven years''.

The ban was strictly enforced and caused much hardship and although it only lasted until 1782 it was enough to kill Highland dress as everyday wear.

When it was repealed there was great rejoicing in the north. A proclamation said:

"This is bringing before all the sons of the Gael, that the King and Parliament of Britain have for ever abolished the Act against the Highland dress: which came down to the Clans from the beginning of the world to the year 1746. This must bring great joy to every Highland heart. You are no longer bound down to the unmanly dress of the Lowlander. This is declaring to every man, young and old, simple and gentle, that they may after this put on and wear the truis, the little Kilt, the coat, and the striped hose, as also the belted plaid, without fear of the law of the realm or the spite of enemies."

So the kilt returned and is still with us to this day.

In telling some of the stories of the Clans I have not tried to give a comprehensive Clan history in each case, but merely a story about each with the whole, hopefully, giving the over-all flavour. Some readers might not like the tale attached to their particular Clan but I have endeavoured to represent a variety of events, stories,and experiences.

In any event, taking offence on behalf of the Clan is a response which itself has valid historical roots!

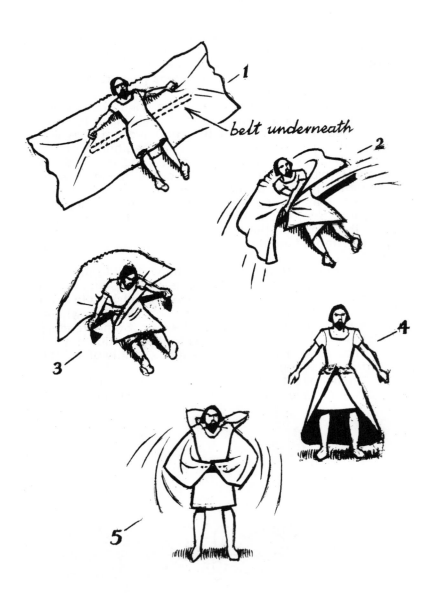

belt underneath

Our artist gives one other version on how the Great Kilt was donned

Your Clan from your name...?

Pinning down one's correct links with a Clan via one's surname can sometimes be very difficult. If you are a MacKenzie or a MacRae then your ancestors clearly came from the Clan lands in Kintail, if a Cameron then your roots lie in Lochaber, if a MacQuarrie then from the island of Ulva, near Mull.

Mac means, of course, "son of", as with the Irish "O' " or Welsh "Fitz", but surnames as we know them today were not in general use in Scotland before the 17th century. People received their names in a variety of ways, son-of-Colin for example, or the name of their locality or estate, or because of their colour. Roy derives from red (ruadh), Dow from dhu (black) or from skills and trades, Miller or Wright or Smith. Some derive from Norse or Norman roots.

Many Clansmen were related by blood to the Chief and his family, others were not and the so-called Sept names attached to Clans, which are not the names of the chief or of the clan, have a variety of origins, population-movement, small families who sought protection by more powerful ones, or were absorbed, the names of trades and crafts, of physical appearance, but they considered themselves part of the Clan - and were so — and people nowadays rightly look for Sept names in that light.

An additional complication in researching ancestry is that some Sept names can be legitimately attached to more than one Clan. Not all people called White, for example, are automatically linked to the MacGregors. To complicate matters further, spelling in past centuries was exceedingly 'loose' and English-speaking clerks sometimes set down the phoenetic spelling of a Gaelic name they only partially grasped and this can make research difficult. The American Cahoon instead of Colquhoun is an example.

My own name, MacOwan, has been spelled by my own ancestors as McCowan and McEwan in past centuries and in parish registers and documentation going back to 1787. It means son of Ewan and as further researches take the male line back to Loch Fyne-side, Argyll, that is where my own Clan roots lie, with the Clan Ewan, of the lands of Otter (from a Gaelic word meaning a spit of land), later to be absorbed by the Campbells. My mother's Clan side of the family is easily traced; she was a Ross, with Gunn on her mother's side.

The Scottish Ancestry Research Society, a national charity based at 3 Albany Street, Edinburgh, have a deserved reputation for research work of integrity, free from guesswork and 'romance'.

So, in tracing a Sept name, one can safely assume that some names have a long connection with an area, and (as with the McMasters being linked to Clan Cameron) have a proven Clan link and were part of the whole. Some others require more research.

Clan links can be long. I was intrigued to be told by Brigadier Ian Stewart, of Achnacone, Appin, who commanded the Argyll and Sutherland Highlanders in Malaya during the Second World War, that he had used bugles and the pipes to pass messages and orders in the jungle as they had no radio sets.

The Argylls fought bravely before being overwhelmed in a disastrous campaign which ended in the fall of Singapore to the Japanese and tributes to them were paid both by their Japanese opponents and by Field Marshall Wavell.

When Brigadier Stewart wanted his men to block a particular section of a road he got his pipe-major to play the old march of the Stewarts of Appin, "We Will Take and Hold the High Road".

In the following sections I have given the main Sept names in each case, an area where there has been much research.

It should not be forgotten, too, that some people in past centuries spontaneously attached themselves to the Clan of their choice, and if you decide to do that there is some historical basis for such a decision.

CLAN BRUCE

Motto -"Fuimus" ("We have been".)

Plant Badge - Rosemary.

Territory - Mainly Annandale and Nithsdale in south-west Scotland, Clackmannan and its fringes and Airth, in Central Scotland.

Sept Names - None, other than the ancient spelling Brus.

THE name Bruce is not Highland but Norman in origin and possibly Norse before that and, strictly speaking, the Bruces are a 'family' rather than a Clan.

King David I granted the Border zone of Annandale to a Robert Bruce in 1124, and Scotland's most famous King, Robert Bruce, came from a family that had been in Scotland for five centuries when he made his bid for the disputed Scottish crown in the 14th century Wars of Independence against the invading and occupation armies of Edward I and Edward II of England.

Bruce is one of Scotland's great heroes. At a time when the nation's fortunes seemed lost, he saw his wife, daughter and sister imprisoned in England, another sister hung in a cage outside a castle wall, and three brothers executed, but he overcame powerful enemies at home, attracted thousands to Scotland's cause and eventually triumphed at the Battle of Bannockburn in 1314 when Edward II's army was crushingly defeated and Scotland's nationhood was secure.

It is worth stating that he is Robert Bruce, King of Scots, not of Scotland (similarly with Mary, Queen of Scots.)

The King was the second man up...

There was a degree of consent among the people to the monarch's rule and the Scots, in their famous (independence) Declaration of Arbroath in 1320, sent to Pope John XXII, who acted rather like a one-man United Nations, said that much as the Scots revered their king (the good Robert, they called him) they would depose even him if he were ever to abandon the fight for Scotland's independence.

Bruce was a man of great passions. He slew one of his rivals, the Red Comyn, before the altar in Greyfriars Kirk, Dumfries, when they met to discuss their differences, but it is his tenacity and bravery that Scots so admire.

Everyone knows the story of Bruce and the spider and how he was inspired by the sight of the insect building and rebuilding its web no matter how many times it was broken.

But he had compassion, too, and it is recorded he once halted his army's progress so that a poor woman could give birth in conditions of safety and care.

He conducted guerilla warfare in our hills and forests, suffered defeats, privation and hardship, but he eventually won through and held his throne and Scotland for many years.

He was a tough and skilled fighter and the poet Barbour's epic saga, "The Bruce" (Scots familiarly say 'Bruce' or 'The Bruce') tells of how the King courageously fought off enemies who almost captured him.

At the Battle of Dalrigh, near Tyndrum, in Strath'fillan, when his small force was defeated in the period after he had been crowned at Scone in defiance of Edward and the Scottish nobles who resisted Bruce's claim to the throne, he just managed to evade his would-be captors, but his plaid brooch, the famous Brooch of Lorn, was literally torn from his clothing by the hostile MacDougalls. The MacDougalls, of course, suffered greatly when Bruce ultimately triumphed for he gave much of their land to the Campbells.

In modern, military parlance, Bruce led from the front. One of his most courageous deeds occurred when he had besieged the town of Perth for six weeks but was short of siege artillery and as the town was well protected by walls and a moat it could not easily be stormed.

Bruce himself during the dark winter nights secretly sounded the depth of the moat until he found a place that

Robert the Bruce, King of Scots — The Victor of Bannockburn

was not much over five feet deep. At New Year he raised the siege and the defenders, mainly Scots who opposed Bruce, jeered as Bruce's men marched away.

They hid in the nearby forests for a week making scaling ladders and remained undetected.

Then, one dark night, Bruce silently led his men back to the moat's edge. He took a ladder and dropped into the water and, carrying his weapons, he felt his way slowly forward using his lance to test the depth.

Barbour says a French Knight who fought with the Scots

was full of admiration for this King wading slowly forward, up to his neck in icy, foul water.

He, too, followed and the rest of Bruce's Scots did the same.

The ladders were set against the wall and the King was the second man up. He divided his men, some to act as a rear-guard for the ladder heads, if that should be necessary, the rest for attack. But the garrison were taken by surprise and most surrendered after some early casualties.

The King ordered the walls to be razed and the moat to be filled in, and by capturing Perth he had cleared Scotland to the Forth.

Ahead lay more successes.

Bruce's great sword was handed to his descendants. On August 26, 1787, Mrs Bruce of Clackmannan used it to "knight" the poet Robert Burns, and it is still in the possession of the modern chief of Clan Bruce, the Earl of Elgin and Kincardine.

CLAN CAMERON

Motto - "Aonaibh richeile" ("Unite".)

Plant Badge - Oak or Crowberry.

Territory - Lochaber, the area around Fort William; Loch Eil, Loch Lochy, Glen Loy, Glen Nevis, Glen Dessary, Glen Pean, Loch Arkaigside.

Sept Names : MacGillonie, MacMartin, MacSorley, Chalmers, MacPhail, MacUlric, Paul, Clark, Taylor, MacChlery.

THE Camerons were always great warriors, holding the boundary lines of their lands with tenacity, particularly against the MacIntoshes, and they were staunch Jacobites. Their name is said to derive from the Gaelic Chamshron, meaning wry-nose, and their war-slogan was, appropriately, "Sons of the hounds, come here and get flesh".

Their history is peppered with the names of great warriors, particularly Donald Dubh (Black Donald) who led the clan in the army of the Lord of the Isles at Harlaw in 1411, and Sir Ewen of Lochiel, chief in 1647 and a thorn in the flesh of Cromwell's Commonwealth in Scotland.

They fought at Killiecrankie with John Graham of Claverhouse, "Bonnie Dundee", in 1689, and were 'out' in the 1715 Jacobite Rising.

The 'gentle Lochiel' of the '45 played a decisive role in that final bid of the Stuarts to regain the throne of Britain. If Clan Cameron had not risen, and taken 800 men to join Prince Charles Edward Stuart the Rising would have fizzled out. Contingents of MacMillans, who lived in Lochaber, also fought with the Camerons.

If Clan Cameron had not risen to support Prince Charles Edward Stuart the rising would have fizzled out...

Lochiel was wounded at Culloden and went into exile. He stopped Glasgow from being sacked by the Jacobite Army and to this day if Cameron of Lochiel visits that city church bells are rung.

His brother, Dr.Archie Cameron, was hanged at Tyburn on June 7, 1753, the last man in Britain to be executed for Jacobitism - he had returned to Scotland from France, reputedly to recover Prince Charlie's gold which is rumoured to lie buried by the shores of Loch Arkaig, and was captured further south.

Here is a story of Sir Ewen, 17th of Lochiel, who became chief in 1647, which typifies Cameron fighting prowess.

Cromwell appointed General George Monk governor in Scotland but he found the Clans a hot handful, particularly the Camerons who had fought with Montrose to try and win Scotland for Charles I.

General Monck built a fort at Inverlochy, landing materials by sea and as Lochiel was away at that time the fort was well advanced by the time he returned.

He had spies working inside and kept a group of 32 of his best warriors hidden at Achdalieu and waited his chance.

When over 130 soldiers were cutting timber in Achdalieu wood the Camerons attacked. The English soldiers had muskets and bayonets but fired too soon and did not have time to reload before the Camerons were in among them with broadswords, dirks, targes, bows and arrows and muskets.

The garrison took terrible casualties and despite their numbers were broken up and retreated.

Lochiel got separated from his men and fought a desperate sword dual with an English officer, finally prising the sword from his grasp.

But the officer, very bravely, wrestled Lochiel to the ground. Clutched together they rolled down a slope and fell into the bed of a dried out burn, with the officer on top.

Both were almost exhausted but the officer managed to get a dagger out and was only prevented by the tight space and Lochiel's arms from stabbing him.

In a bid to launch a proper blow, the officer raised himself up. As he did so, Lochiel caught him by the collar and sunk his teeth into his neck, taking away a mouthful of flesh. The pain-stricken officer lost his grip and was quickly despatched.

Lochiel was to narrowly survive twice more. As the retreating soldiers tried to regain their boats one of them shot at Lochiel who saw him at the last second and dived into deep water to avoid the shot.

Another, resting his musket on the gunwale as the Camerons attacked the boats, aimed at Lochiel but his foster-brother threw himself in front of his chief and received the shot in his own chest.

There is, reputedly, a sequel to this story. Some years later when Sir Ewen was in London he went to a barber to be shaved before going to court.

As the razor was passed over his throat the barber asked - "Are you from the North, Sir?"

Sir Ewen admitted he was. "Do you know people from the North?" he replied. "No", said the barber, "nor do I wish to, they are savages there.

"Would you believe it, sir - one of them tore the throat out of my father with his teeth, and I only wish I had that fellow's throat as near me as yours is now."

Clansmen, telling the story, remarked that their chief avoided barbers after that.

CLAN CAMPBELL

Motto - "Ne obliviscaris" ("Forget Not").

Plant Badge - Wild myrtle, fir club moss.

Territory - Argyllshire, reaching eastwards to Loch Earn and Loch Tay, north to Appin, Glen Coe and Loch Rannoch, the Tarbert isthmus just north of Kintyre, the peninsula between Loch Fyne and the Firth of Clyde. The Campbells also held the Ayrshire lands of the Earls of Loudoun and land between the rivers Nairn and Findhorn, in the north-east, held by the Campbells of Cawdor.

Sept names - Burnhouse, Burns, Connochie, Denoon, MacConnochie, MacDiarmid, MacGibbon,

MacIsaac, MacKellar, MacKessock, MacOran, Mac-
Phedran, MacUre, Ure, (all of Campbell of Argyll and
Breadalbane). Caddell is a Sept of Cawdor. Names that
were separate clans are also associated with the Campbells, such as MacArthur and McEwan.

CLAN Campbell's name can still arouse strong emotions
ranging from cries of cruelly-ambitious, unscrupulous,
greedy, treacherous and traitorous on the one hand to
powerful, sensible, politically sensitive, level-headed,
successful, on the other. It all depends on your point of
view.

Possibly excluding the Gordons, they were the most
powerful clan in Scotland, able to put thousands of men
under arms, and with many influential cadet-houses. The
name derives from the Gaelic cam-beul, crooked mouth,
and their war-cry or slogan was "Cruachan", that splendid, many-topped mountain which dominates Loch Awe.

Their chiefs had the knack, on the whole, (there are
exceptions) of associating themselves successfully with
lowland nobles, monarchs and the government of the day
and were perhaps alone of the Gaelic clans in being able
to do this. They tended to prefer litigation to acquire land
or deal with enemies, rather than the sword. They were
winners.

Originally known as Clan Diarmid their chiefs took
the title MacCailein Mor, son of Colin the Great, from the
heroic Sir Colin Campbell who died fighting for Bruce in
the Scottish Wars of Independence. His son also supported Bruce and Campbell power and lands increased
vastly as a result.

There is not space here to give a detailed account of
Campbell history but they 'acquired' MacDonald lands in
Knapdale, then Kintyre, then nibbled away at the
MacLeans in Mull, Morvern, Tiree and Coll, and spread
elsewhere.

Occasionally they slipped up - two chiefs were executed, one for opposing James VII, but they energetical-
ly opposed the Jacobites and are popularly regarded as a
Hanoverian clan. In fairness to those whose sympathies
lie with the Jacobites, it must be said that some Campbells supported the exiled King James in the 1715 Rising
and that there were contingents of Campbells on both
sides at Culloden in 1746. Author Neil Munro's historical
novels "John Splendid" and "The New Road", are ex-

cellent reads, with the Campbells as 'goodies'.

Their original stronghold was Ardconnell Castle on Inchconnell island on Loch Awe, and the present day Inverary Castle - the Campbell capital - was built in the 19th century.

Of the great Campbell houses there is space here to deal only with one, Glenorchy or Breadalbane. The Breadalbane motto is "Follow Me" (Cawdor's is "Be Mindful").

An interesting tale, however, states that a younger son of the 2nd Earl of Argyll, Sir John Campbell, kidnapped and married Muriel, heiress of the ancient Thanes of Cawdor, in 1510. The present Cawdor Castle dates back to 1454 and legend has it that the thane fastened a casket of gold on to a donkey's back and said he would build a castle where it halted. The donkey stopped at a hawthorn tree and a castle was built there. A hawthorn tree can still be seen in a vault.

The Campbells of Glenorchy (later Earls and Marquesses of Breadalbane) became very powerful and their lands stretched from East Perthshire to the coast of Argyll. One of their best known chiefs was "Black Duncan", 7th of Glenorchy, who built or renovated seven castles to hold his lands. Here is one story about that family.

Sir Colin Campbell, known as "Caliean Dubh na Roimhe" (Black Colin of Rome), received the lands of Glenorchy after the MacGregors had been driven out.

He was Lord of Kilchurn Castle, on Loch Awe, whose massive walls can still be seen, and he became a Knight-Templar, one of the great military orders of the Middle Ages.

They endeavoured to keep a free passage for Christian pilgrims going to the Holy Land and fought against the Saracens in the Crusades.

Sir Colin knew he would be away for some years so he arranged that men from his clan who accompanied him would return from time to time and let Lady Campbell and his young son know how he was getting on.

When he was in Rome he had an odd dream which so disturbed him that he told a monk about it and the monk advised him to return home.

He made the long way back to Scotland, disguised as a beggar, his mind both anxious and elated because he had been away for seven years.

He sought shelter at a place called Succoth where an old woman lived who had once been his nurse.

Still in disguise, he asked for shelter and food and she let him come and sit by the fire.

When he stretched out his hands to the flames she saw a scar on his arm which had been there since infancy and she recognised him.

She was overjoyed and told the startled Sir Colin that he had been reported dead.

No messengers or letter had arrived home for years, and word had circulated that Sir Colin had been killed in battle.

All the tales had come from a neighbouring laird, Baron McCorquodale, who had imprisoned or killed all Sir Colin's messengers.

Not only that, but Lady Campbell firmly believed her husband dead for several years. The Baron had proposed marriage to her and she, living in a cruel age and desiring protection, had eventually agreed.

Sir Colin was just in time. The wedding had been fixed for the next day.

Still in his beggar's rags he set out for Kilchurn and secretly crossed the drawbridge among a crowd of other people. The pipes played, people sang, food and drink were served to all.

A servant asked him what he needed and he said he wanted both his hunger and thirst satisfied.

Food was immediately served but he insisted that the lady of the castle give him a cup with her own hands.

Silence fell as word spread about this strange beggar and Lady Campbell came forward, mystified, but benevolently disposed and presented him with a cup of wine.

He drank her health and, as he handed the empty cup back, dropped a ring into it.

When she picked it out she went deathly pale and the company crowded forward to see what was happening. She had given that ring to her husband when he departed on the Crusades and which he promised to wear at all times.

"Where did you get tnis", she demanded "Where did you find it? How did my husband die?"

Sir Colin replied - "I got it from you on our parting day and I gave it to you on our wedding day".

Bruce

Campbell

Cameron

Chattan

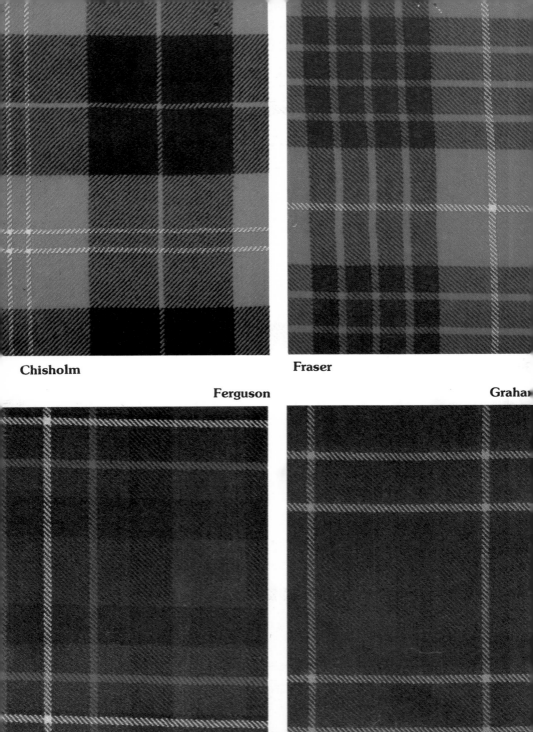

Chisholm

Fraser

Ferguson

Graha

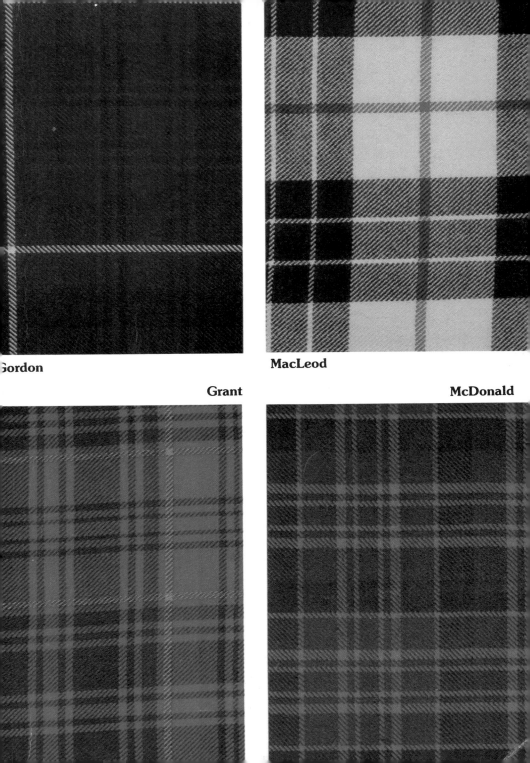

Gordon

MacLeod

Grant

McDonald

McGregor

McLean of Duart

McKenzie

Stewar

Sir Colin still had on the white coat of the Knight-Templar with the scarlet cross on the breast.

He threw off his beggar's cloak, and dishevelled and travel-dirty though he was, with unkempt hair and grimy face, he still had on the white cloak of the Knight-Templar with the scarlet cross on the breast.

The crowd gasped, then cheers rent the air. Lady Campbell, close to fainting, embraced him, the piper struck up joyful tunes and in the tumult Baron McCorquodale was able to slip away.

Sir Colin let him go unpunished but not so his son, Black Colin, who after his father's death took the Baron's lands from him forever.

CLAN CHATTAN

Motto - "Touch not the cat but (without) a glove".

Plant Badge - Red Wortleberry (the Macphersons is white heather)

Territory - Clan Chattan is the name for a federation of Clans; The **Mackintosh** lands were bounded on the west by a line runing south from Inverness to a point north of Newtonmore, then north-east along the River Findhorn, bordering the MacPhersons and Grants, and thence north-west to the Moray Firth. The **MacBains** held lands in the north-west at Kinchyle, south of Inverness, and near Tomatin. The **MacGillivrays** held Dunmaglass in Strathnairn, and the **MacPhersons** held sway in wide Badenoch. The **Farquharsons** seat of power was Invercauld, near Braemar, and the **MacThomas** lands were in Glen Shee.

Sept Names · Clan MacIntosh; Adamson, Clark, Clarkson, Crerar, Dallas, Elder, Glennie, Hardie, MacClerich, Macglashan, MacNiven, MacRitchie, Noble, Shaw, Tarrill, Tosh.

Clan MacPherson; Cattanach, Clark, Currie, Gillespie, Gillies, Gow, Lees, MacGowan, MacLeish, MacVurrich, Murdoch.

Clan Shaw; MacHay, Adamson, Esson, Sheath,.

Clan MacBean; Bain, Bean, MacBeth, MacVean,.

Clan Farquharson; Coutts, Farquhar, Findlay, Hardie, Lyon, MacCaig, MacEaracher, MacKerracher, Riach.

Clan MacPhail; MacFaul, Fall, McPaul.

Clan Davidson; Davie, Davis, Dawson, Dow, MacDade, Kay.

Clan MacGillivray; Gilroy, Macilroy, MacGilvrg.

Clan MacQueen; MacCunn, MacSwan, MacSween.

Clan MacThomas; Combe, Combie, McColn, McComish, , Tam, Thom, Thomas, Thoms, Thomson.

The Clan Chattan is one of the great 'alliances' of Clan history in Scotland, and MacIntosh is generally regarded as the over-all chief although this has been disputed on occasion.

The origin of MacIntosh is **Clann-an-Toisich,** from **Mac-an- toisich,** Son of the Thane; their war-cry or slogan was **"Loch Moigh!"** (Loch Moy). MacPherson is derived from **Mac-a-Phearsoin,** son of the parson, and the Gaelic name is **Clann Mhuirich.** The MacPhersons' slogan is **"Creagan Dubh!"** (The Black Rock).

As befits clans with the fierce insignia of the wild cat, they were in many a battle. They fought in the '15 and the '45, at Red Harlaw in 1411, in the last inter-clan battle at Mulroy in 1688 where they had a boundary dispute with the MacDonnells of Keppoch, and many another.

In the 15th century they had a dispute with the Comyns over the possession of Castle Rait, and the Comyns invited the Macintoshes to the castle to discuss peace. But a Comyn lad was in love with a Macintosh girl whom he asked to meet him at the Grey Stone, or Listening Stone, near the church of Croy. He told her that when a bull's head would be brought into the feast the Comyns would fall upon their Macintosh guests. So the Macintoshes went prepared with dirks hidden in their clothing. When the bull's head was brought in they instantly attacked the Comyns and regained possession of the castle. It's known as getting your retaliation in first.

In the time of King Robert III bad feeling betwen Clan Chattan and the Camerons reached such a pitch that they were asked to select 30 warriors to fight it out in front of the King at the North Inch, Perth, in 1396.

The Clan Chattan unexpectedly found themselves a man short on the day and a harness-maker or armourer-smith who had turned up to see the fun made up the vacancy. He fought bravely and was later adopted in the Clan and the sept of Gower Smith is said to derive from that. Clan Chattan won and had 11 survivors, the Camerons were all slain but for one man who jumped into the River Tay and got away. That ended the feuding for many years.

The '45 Jacobite Rising brought fame to a remarkable woman, redoubtable "Colonel Anne".

A Farquharson of Invercauld, and an ardent Jacobite, she was married to the Chief of Macintosh who decided not to 'come out' to support the cause of Prince Charles Edward Stuart.

There must have been some brisk pillow-talk in that house because he continued to hold his military commission under the Hanoverian King George II and commanded a company of the Black Watch, the Highland militia raised on behalf of the Government to curb cattle-reiving and to keep law and order and so called because of their dark tartan.

She was only 20 but she raised the Clan to fight for the Prince. She selected MacGillivray of Dunmaglass as its colonel and on the first formal parade she inspected the clansmen wearing a man's bonnet, a tartan riding habit and carrying pistols at her saddle-bow.

Later in the campaign she received Prince Charlie at Moy Hall and at one point he was almost trapped by Hanoverian soldiers moving from Inverness.

She sent Donald Fraser, the smith at Moy, and four other men to watch the road and at midnight they heard the Hanoverian troops approaching.

Fraser put his men among peat-stacks in the hope they might be mistaken in the darkness for groups of men. They fired their guns, shouted several clan slogans, darted from one point to another, and the soldiers thinking they faced a sizable force hastily retreated. The clash became known as the Rout of Moy, and the smith's sword and anvil can still be seen at Moy Hall.

"Colonel Anne" was treated roughly by the Hanoverian
soldiers.

Ironically, when Jacobite Clansmen later took the Chief of Macintosh prisoner after a skirmish with Hanoverian forces, the Prince sent him back to his own wife at Moy saying he could not be in better security or more honoroubly treated.

So "Colonel Anne" had to put her own husband under house-arrest.

Sadly, the Macintosh regiment suffered severe casualties at Culloden, and the Rising was put down with great cruelty.

When Hanoverian soldiers reached Moy Hall they initially treated her roughly, striking her and demanding money. Later she was taken to Inverness and put under house arrest and reasonably well treated.

But there was to be a sequel. Two years later she visited London and attended a ball given by the William, Duke of Cumberland, the King's son who had put down the Rising and who was directly responsible for orders which led to the killing of wounded men, executions, house-burning and much persecution.

He asked her to dance, and the tune played was "Up and waur (worst) them a' Willie". She asked him coldly that as she had danced to his tune would he, now, dance to hers. As the host, he agreed.

Amid a shocked and, in some cases, admiring silence, she asked for "The Auld (old) Stuarts Back Again", and like it or not, that was the tune they danced to.

But there was to be a sequel. Two years later she visited London and attended a ball given by William, Duke of Cumberland, the King's son who had put down the Rising and who was directly responsible for orders which led to the killing of wounded men, executions, house-burning and much persecution.

He asked her to dance, and the tune played was "Up and waur (worst) them a', Willie". She asked him coldly that as she had danced to his tune would he, now, dance to hers. As the host, he agreed.

Amid a shocked and, in some cases, admiring silence, she asked for "The Auld (old) Stuarts Back Again", and like it or not, that was the tune they danced to.

CLAN CHISHOLM

Motto - "Feros Ferio" ("I am fierce with the fierce".)
Plant Badge - Fern
Territory - In the north-west Highlands, west of Inverness, Loch Affric to Comar, bounded on the west by the MacKenzie lands of Kintail. To the north lay the Frasers, to the south-east the Grants. Fraser lands in Strathglass separated Chisholm territory at Comar and Erchless. There were also Border Chisholmes, and at Cromlix, in Perthshire.
Sept Names - Possibly Aird.

The Chisholms were of Norman origin and their lands in the glens of the rivers Glass, Affric and Cannich, and around Loch Affric, beautifully wooded, are among the loveliest areas in the Highlands. It is said that a Chisholm chief remarked that only three individuals in the world were entitled to be described by the definite article, The Pope, The King and The Chisholm. The Gaelic name is **Clann Siosal.**

They were never a big Clan and could only put around 200 men under arms and were surrounded by more powerful clans.

But they had plenty of spirit, and were well sprinkled with men of resolve both in war and peace. The house of Cromlix produced three Catholic bishops at the time of the Reformation and three Chisholms were among the famous Seven Men of Glen Moriston (who actually numbered eight) who gave shelter to the fugitive Prince Charles Edward Stuart when he was on the run in the West Highlands.

In the years of relative peace following the failure of the 1715 and 1719 Jacobite Risings, some Clans reached an uneasy 'settlement' with the Hanoverian government.

James and John found the body of Roderick Og

When the '45 broke out MacIan chief of the Chisholms, was to old to "come out" in support of the Stuart cause and by that time two of his five sons, John and James, held commissions in the Hanoverian Army, in the Royal Scots Regiment.

This is the tragic story of a divided family because at the Battle of Culloden in 1746, the last land battle on British soil, the Chisholms in the Jacobite Army were led by the youngest son, Roderick Og, while 600 yards away across the moor his brothers stood in the enemy ranks. With him was Ian Beg, piper to the Chisholms, who stood behind his young Colonel and held the clan's legendary Black Chanter, known as "The Maiden of the Sandal". It had been brought from Rome by a chief and bound with hoops of silver by later chiefs.

It was reputed to have supernatural powers and if a member of the chief's family was about to die, no man could finger a note from it, and no note was played that day.

The story of Culloden is well known. The Jacobite Clans, once so brilliantly led, were now poorly directed. Sizable contingents were on duty elsewhere. Many of the men were tired and hungry as a result of poor staff work and the called-off night attack plan on Cumberland's camp. They stood in ranks being systematically shelled and shot at before, galled, they charged into a hail of fire and suffered huge casualties.

Roderick Og was struck down by a cannon ball just before the charge and was being carried to the rear when he was struck again, this time fatally.

The Chisholms suffered many dead and wounded in the charge and the moor was thick with corpses.

The Royal Scots had by now been moved to another position and Captain James Chisholm and Captain John Chisholm did not see, because of dust and smoke, what had happened to their brother and kinsmen on the other side.

When it was all over, and the Hanoverian army moved forward, killing the wounded, or leaving them untended, James and John found the body of Roderick.

They cleaned his face and straightened his limbs and guarded the body so it would not be mutilated.

In terms of the continuance of the Gaelic or Clans way of life this example of divided family loyalties had no winners.

When the 19th century Highland clearances took place the Chisholms particularly suffered and hundreds were forced to migrate to Cape Breton, and Antigonish in Nova Scotia and to Glengarry in Canada, and their beautiful glens are now relatively empty.

CLAN DONALD

Warcry or Slogan - **"Fraoch Eilean"** ("The Heathery Isle").

Plant Badge - Heather.

Territory - Dealt with under the main branches.

Sept Names - Include, Beaton, Beith, Bowie, Connall, Darroch, Donald, Donaldson, Gilbride, Galbraith, Gerrie, Gowrie, Hewison, Houston, Hutcheson, Johnson, Kellie, Kinnell, Kinniburgh, MacBride, MacConnell, MacCutcheon, MacGeachie, MacEachern, MacHugh, Macilwraith, MacIan, McIlwraith, MacKelloch, MacRory, May, Murchison, O'May, Purcell, Revie and Shannon.

Sept names for Clanranald include Allan, Allanson, Currie, MacAllan, MacGeachie, MacKechnie, MacIsaac; Glen Garry names include Alexander and Sanderson; Keppoch names include Philipson, MacKillop.

What can one say about the great Clan Donald, the largest of all the Highland clans, that would not take volumes?

It is significant that the origin of the name is the Gaelic **Domhnull,** world ruler, and the Gaelic name for the clan is **Clann Dhomnuill.**

The MacDonalds have their ancestors in the renowned Lords of the Isles who were as powerful as Scottish Kings.

They also at one stage held the Isle of Man and also became Earls of Ross and were the great rivals of the Campbells.

They produced the famous Somerled who brilliantly fought the Norsemen and was himself slain by King Malcolm IV in 1164.

One of his grandsons, Donald, gave his name to the whole clan. The clan were divided in the Scottish Wars of Independence but most supported Bruce and prospered accordingly. They spread to Antrim, in Ireland, and in 1354 defied the Scots Crown, maintaining the independence of the Lord of the Isles but found that title annexed to the Crown a century later (Prince Charles now holds it).

The MacDougalls sprang from their line, but eventually became a separate Clan.

The Clan Donald spread into eight main branches (seven in later centuries) and nowadays three are regarded as paramount, or the most interesting, Macdonald of Sleat (pronounced slate) on Skye, Macdonald of Clanranald and Macdonald of Glengarry. At Armadale, on Skye, there is now an absorbing museum to Clan Donald which is well worth a visit.

James IV, towards the end of the 16th century, tried to make the Highland chiefs and Border leaders responsible for their clans and followers but no one man could be found to be answerable for Clan Donald. Six were named and in later years Sleat, Clanranald and Glengarry were paramount.

Although not all MacDonalds supported Prince Charles Edward Stuart, many did, particularly those of Clanranald, Glengarry and Keppoch.

When the Captain of Clanranald fell at Sheriffmuir in 1715 the Laird of Glengarry shouted: "Revenge today and mourning tomorrow..."

Miss Flora Macdonald

Their story is larded with heroic men and women...it was Ranald Macdonald, chief of Clanranald who met Bonnie Prince Charlie on his arrival in Moidart. He was later hunted as a fugitive, dodged the Redcoats, escaped to France and ended up aide-de-camp to Marshal de Saxe...Alastair Macdonnell of Glengarry was the last Highland chief to live in the old style and is reputed to be the original of Sir Walter Scott's Fergus MacIvor in his novel "Waverley"...the Glengarry Macdonnells were insulted at being placed on the left wing at Culloden in 1746, instead of their honoured place on the right, butthey fought with their usual resolution...The poor MacDonalds of Glen Coe, who in 1692, were the victims of the infamous massacre when their Campbell guests broke their trust and turned on their hosts, and whose men fought so valiantly for the Jacobite cause...During the Scottish Wars of the Covenant, the Marquis of Montrose's second-in-command was the feared Colkitto MacDonald who, it is persuasively argued, was the military genius behind their whirlwind campaign in 1645...Marshall MacDonald, Duke of Taranto, became one of Napoleon's generals and, it is said, was not allowed too near Highland troops in the British Army in case the sound of the pipes made him forget his allegiance to the French...Flora MacDonald who risked her life to hide Bonnie Prince Charlie.The roll call could go on and on.

The motto of the Macdonalds of Sleat, Glengarry and Keppoch is "per mare per terra" ("By sea and by land") and Clanranald's is "My hope is constant in thee" (a comment made by Bruce at Bannockburn).

The slogan of Clan Donald is **"Fraoch Eilean"** (The Heathery Isle), but Clanranald have **"Dh'aindeoin co' Theireadh e!"** ("Gainsay who dare"), Glengarry **"Creagan-an-Fhithich"** ("The Raven's Rock") and Keppoch **"Dia's Naomh Aindrea"** ("God and St.Andrew").

Territory included Kintyre, Ardnamurchan, Glen Coe, Glengarry, Knoydart, Morar, Arisaig, Islay, Keppoch (Lochaber), Lochalsh, Uist, Benbecula, Rum, Eigg, Muck, part of Jura, Moidart, Sleat (Skye), Trotternish (Skye) and Antrim (Ulster).

One story must suffice for this great Clan and it is how the famous Somerled tricked his enemies into thinking he had three armies at his immediate command.

Many centuries ago Scotland's north and west coasts were harassed by the Norsemen, Viking raiders from Scandinavia who were expert sailors and doughty warriors.

They formed settlements and eventually controlled Orkney, Shetland, and parts of the Western Isles, Sutherland (the 'south land' to the Norsemen) and Caithness.

They even spread into mainland Argyll, and Somerled and his father, Gilbert, found themselves fugitives in their own land.

Gilbert was too old to fight but Somerled brooded angrily over his inability to throw out the invaders. Then a strange event happened.

The Norsemen had a battle with the Clan McInnes and slew their chief.
Leaderless, they agreed to find a new chief who was warlike and one story even says that they decided to ask the first suitable man they met by chance. That man was Somerled, fishing disonsolately at the mouth of a burn on the shores of Loch Linnhe.

They invited him to be their war leader but before he answered Somerled got a tug on his line. He had hooked a salmon. He told the McInnes clansmen that if he landed the fish he would agree to be their leader.

They watched, enthralled, as he battled to land the salmon with his tiny rod. Eventually, it lay flapping on the bank.

So the demoralised MacInnes' had a new leader. Somerled asked for, and got, a solemn oath that they would obey his commands.

He told them to light many fires round their encampment to give the impression of large numbers of men. He then hurried back to the cave where his father had taken refuge, cooked the salmon for his meal, saw to his needs, and hurried back to join the MacInnes' warriors.

Next day he lay in the heather and watched the Viking longships land hundreds of men. His own force was outnumbered so he knew that only bluff would work.

He told the MacInnes Clansmen to kill a herd of cattle in a nearby glen and to skin them.

He ordered his small band on to a prominent knoll so that the Vikings could see them, and then to descend, march round the base of the hill and back to the top again, giving the impression of a long continuous column of

Somerled headed his force in a yelling charge and cut down many of the Vikings.

armed warriors.

He then asked them to do the same wearing the cattle hides with the smooth side out.

The eagle-eyed Norsemen thought he had summoned up another band, and they halted their advance inland and looked warily towards the high ground on which Somerled had his men.

Somerled then made them march around a third time with the rough side of the hides showing.

The Norsemen thought a third band had gathered and began to fall back towards their boats. Taking advantage of their indicision and of the sloping ground, Somerled led his small force in a yelling charge and cut down many of the Vikings.

The rest made for the ships and hastily rowed out into mid-loch. The MacInnes men were overjoyed and other men flocked to Somerled's standard. He had many other victories and controlled Lochaber, Morven and northern Argyll. He helped King David II drive the Norsemen from the Isle of Man, Arran and Bute and was given these islands by the King.

He also got control of the Western Isles, then ruled by a Viking called Eric the Red. Somerled carried off his daughter, Ragnhildie, and married her. She did not appear to mind too much.

They had three sons; Dugall was to found the Clan MacDougal, Reginald who inherited Lorn, Jura and Mull, and Angus who was to control Bute and Arran.

It was Reginald, of course, who through his son, Donald, gave his name to the overall Clan, and who took the title 'Lord of the Isles'.

CLAN FERGUSSON

Motto · Dulcius ex asperis ("Sweeter after difficulties").
"Arte et marte", (By Art and Force, is also given).

Plant Badge · Poplar, pine, little sunflower and foxglove.

Territory · Lands in Ayrshire (Kilkerran), Dumfries,
Galloway, Perthshire (Balquhidder, Loch Earn, Comrie;
and near Aberfeldy and Pitlochry), Argyll (Strachur), Aberdeenshire.

Sept Names · Fergus, Ferris, Feris, MacKerras, MacAdie,
MacAdie (Perthshire), MacKersey (Argyll).

Although the Fergussons are nowadays regarded as
one clan their history shows five main branches, with early roots; Fergusson of Kilkerran, Ayrshire, for example, is
descended from Fergus, Prince of Galloway, who died in
1161, and the Argyll branch claims descent from the royal
house of Dalriada.

The Gaelic name is Clann Fhearghuis and the war-cry
or slogan is "Clann Fhearghuis gu brath" ("Clan Fergus
For Ever").

They produced energetic and vigorous leaders and
were rarely absent from the great issues and power struggles in Scotland although with diverse views: most of the
lowland Fergussons were Covenanters, the Atholl
Fergussons supported Montrose in 1645 and were ardent
Jacobites (others supported the Hanoverian cause, in-

They took the Saltire sign as divine favour and won a crushing victory.

cluding the notorious Captain John Fergusson who scoured the Hebrides in his ship "Furnace" for the fugitive Bonnie Prince Charlie and who was responsible for many atrocities.)

If you have ever heard Robert Burns' lovely song "Bonnie Annie Laurie" it is intriguing to note that the lucky husband of Annie Laurie of Maxwelton (they married in 1709) was Alexander Fergusson, 10th of Craigdarroch.

The Fergussons lay claim to being responsible for Scotland having the Saltire, the white diagonal cross on a blue background, as her flag.

Angus (Hungas) MacFergus, a Pictish king descended through his mother from the Dalriadic Fergussons, was a great warrior and in the 9th century extended his overlordship for a time from the Shetlands to the Humber. At Athelstaneford, in East Lothian, his army faced a much larger army of the Northumbrians and their allies. Some legends say Fergus had a dream and saw a white Saltire cross in a blue sky, others say his men saw it themselves in the sky. They took it as divine favour and an excellent omen and won a crushing victory.

Angus MacFergus from then on adopted the white cross and blue background as his own flag and it was eventually to become the flag of all Scotland.

CLAN FRASER

Motto · "Je Suis Prest" ("I Am Ready")

Plant Badge · Yew

Territory · Around Inverness, the Aird district of Inverness-shire, running 30 miles westwards from Inverness along the south shores of the Beauly Firth: Stratherrick, down the south bank,of Loch Ness: Philorth, Aberdeenshire, (the town of Fraserburgh), part of Strathglass and Strathfarrar.

Sept Names · Frizell (an alternative form of Fraser), Tweedie, MacGruer, Simon, Sime, Simpson, MacImmey, MacKin.

The Frasers were a large and powerful clan, particularly the Lovat Frasers, whose chief was styled Mac-Shimidh (son of Simon), and they had several cadet branches.

They produced great soldiers, a tradition that continues into modern times with the formation of the regiment, the Lovat Scouts.

The Frasers were of Norman or Frankish origin and probably descend from a Knight or Knights who came to Scotland to aid Scottish Kings to rule their turbulent kingdoms.

The name is said to derive from the French word "fraise" (strawberry). One story says that Julius de Berry of Bourbon entertained one of the French kings with a dish of strawberries and so incurred his favour that he was later knighted.

52

Strawberries were taken into his coat-of-arms (and are still in the Fraser coat-of-arms with three crowns which were added when one of the Frasers married a niece of King Robert I).

They first settled in Tweedale, then eventually established themselves in the north. In 1537 they founded the town of Fraserburgh and King James VI granted them charters to found a short-lived university (Fraserburgh still has a street called College Bounds). In 1670 the Laird of Philorth inherited the Saltoun peerage and chiefs of the name of Fraser are Earls of Saltoun.

The Fraser lands have many fine lochs and salmon rivers and an old tale says that Lord Lovat once placed a wood fire and a kettle of water on a rock beside the River Beauly. A salmon leaped right out of the water into the pot!

The Frasers also took part in one of the fiercest of Clan battles, The Field of the Shirts.

A young MacDonald of Clanranald was brought up at Castle Dounie, the Fraser stronghold, and he unexpectedly became chief of Clan Ranald, a claim contested by John of Moidart.

He turned out to be a sore disappointment (and at this point Clanranald readers are permitted to go red and become indignant and point to other versions), and tactlessly deplored the arrangements that had been made to give him a fitting reception.

He criticised the numbers of cattle and goats killed for the feast and remarked that "a few hens would have done as well".

His clansmen and women were greatly offended and rejected and ostracised him. He was nick-named "Ranald of the Hens".

However, he must have had spirit because he went straight back to the Frasers and persuaded them to go to war on his behalf, not that they needed too much persuading because the MacDonalds had raided Fraser lands.

The two sides met beside Loch Lochy on a sweltering July day and because the warriors threw off their plaids in the heat, the battle came to be known as "Blar na Leine" (The Field of the Shirts).

It was a dreadful fight over the leadership issue, but Highland pride can be a fearsome thing and many hundreds died. Only ten men on each side were said to have

They filled their bonnets with water and drank a toast to the exiled King James

been left alive. Among the dead was MacShimidh and his heir, a young boy, who reputedly returned to the battlefield after his stepmother accused him of cowardice.

The Frasers were involved in many Scottish power-struggles, and sometimes on opposing sides.

When James VII was dethroned and William of Orange was invited to replace him by the English and some sections of the Scottish population, Lord Tullibardine, the son of the Marquis of Atholl, raised a body of Atholl men which included 300 Frasers.

They paraded at Blair Castle and when their leaders addressed them they realised that they were supposed to support King William.

The Fraser contingent rebelled, left the parade and headed for the nearest burn. They filled their bonnets with water and drank a toast to the exiled King James.

Then off they went to follow John Graham of Claverhouse, "Bonnie Dundee".

They fought bravely under Claverhouse at the battle of Killiecrankie, but Claverhouse was killed and the rising petered out.

It was a clan of characters...Sir Simon Fraser supported the great Scottish guerilla leader, William Wallace, during the Scottish Wars of Independence and was executed in London in 1306...Simon, 11th Lord Lovat, lived in great style and secretly negotiated with the Jacobites (who made him a duke) while professing loyalty to the Hanoverians...He sent his son and 500 men to join Prince Charles Edward Stuart...ultimately his double-dealing caught up with him and he was executed in 1747 at Tower Hill, London, the last man to die by beheading in Britain...in the Second World War Lord Lovat was a distinguished Commando leader.

The Gaelic name of the clan is **Clann Fhriseal**. Beaufort Castle now stands on the site of the old Dounie Castle burned in 1746 and the Clan's slogan is **"Caisteal Dhunaidh"** ("Castle Dounie").

CLAN GORDON

Motto - "Bydand" ("Remaining"). The old motto was "Animo non astutia" ("By Courage Not Craft").

Plant Badge - Ivy.

Territory - In the north-east of Scotland and comprising three main areas, Strathbogie and Enzie (including Huntly Castle and Gordon Castle) stretching into the mountains -Aboyne, Glentanar and Glenmuick on Deeside - and close to the city of Aberdeen.

Sept names - Adam, Adie, Crombie, Edie, Milne, Todd.

Like Clan Campbell and Clan Donald the Gordons were numerous, powerful and prominent in Scottish history. They had a kind of swashbuckling swagger and one of the most popular Scottish dances is called "The Gay Gordons".

The word gay has more than one connotation nowadays and it must be immediately pointed out that it derives from a Scots word **gey** which means self-important (but with lightness with it) or overwhelming . The Queen-Regent, Mary of Guise, in the 17th century, called the Gordons "Cock o' the North", a nickname the Gordons chiefs have had ever since.

The Gordons were originally French in origin and held land in the Borders. (There is a parish of Gordon in Berwickshire). An old tale speaks of a Gordon knight ridding Tweedside of a wild boar which had killed many

Jane, Duchess of Gordon, placed a guinea between her lips and kissed each man as he joined up.

hunters and caused much damage to farms. His bravery resulted in a grant of land and the emblem of the boar's head was assumed as his family's armorial bearings. One of them helped present the famous Declaration of Arbroath before the Pope and King Robert the Bruce rewarded him with lands in the north-east where they spread and prospered.

Their Aberdeen connection (they undertook to protect the city) led to trading links with the Baltic, and a Gordon even ended up as Governor of Kiev, in the Ukraine, having joined the service of the Russian czars.

Their womenfolk, too, had spirit and character. Lady Catherine Gordon in 1496 married Perkin Warbeck, pretender to the English throne who said he was Richard, Duke of York, one of the Princes allegedly murdered in the Tower of London by their uncle Gloucester. Alas, his rising failed and he was hanged. Lady Catherine then caught the eye of the winner, Henry VII, married three times more and was given the title "The White Rose".

They occasionally fell from their proud position. When Charles I was executed, the Earl of Huntly, who had supported him, lost his head as well. He is reported as saying - "You may take my head from my shoulders, but not my heart from my sovereign".

They brought nearly 3000 men to the Jacobite cause in the abortive 1715 Rising but were divided in their loyalties when the '45 came along - however, many of the Clan came 'out' for Prince Charles Edward Stuart.

The famous regiment, the Gordon Highlanders, had its roots in this clan.

An old saying - hotly disputed by other regiments -states "Ye're no' a sodger if ye're no' a Gordon". The regiment was first raised in 1794 by Jane, Duchess of Gordon. She placed a guinea between her lips and kissed each man as he joined up.

They produced some intriguing characters both ancient and modern. One of the Moray lairds, Sir Robert Gordon, was known as the "Warlock Laird of Moray". He was a chemist of a kind and had a laboratory in his house in Gordonstoun but the country people believed his experiments meant he was a sorcerer and in the pay of the Devil.

A cave on the Moray coast is said to have been a smuggling stronghold of the Warlock Laird. He owned a ship called "The Nancy" which liaised with French vessels, took off their contraband and hid them in the cave until a high tide at night meant they could be safely removed.

Sir Walter Scott's famous poem about Young Lochinvar is believed to be based on the southern Gordons. A young Gordon was in love with the daughter of Graeme of Netherby in Cumberland. Her father refused them permission to marry and arranged another marriage for her.

Young Lochinvar rode into England to try and stop the wedding but arrived when the festivities were in full swing. Despite the hostility of her family he joined in, drank a cup of wine, and asked the bride to dance.

Then with a touch to her hand and a word in her ear, they raced to the hall door and then outside where Lochinvar's horse was waiting. He vaulted into the saddle, helped the bride up behind him and was off!

"There was mounting 'mong Graemes of the Netherby Clan,
Fosters, Fenwicks and Musgraves they rode and they ran.
There was racing and chasing on Canonbie Lee,
But the lost bride of Netherby ne'er did they see!
So daring in love and dauntless in war,
Have ye e'er heard of gallant like Young Lochinvar?"

There was gallantry, too, from a Gordon in more recent centuries in Charles George Gordon who died in the Sudanese town of Khartoum. He was a regular soldier, fought in the Crimean War and then so distinguished himself in Wars in China that the Emperor offered him enormous sums of money to join his service. But he refused and became Governor of the Egyptian Equatorial Provinces where he strove to stamp out the slave trade.

In 1884, as Governor of the Sudan, he returned to Khartoum where the city was besieged by a fanatical army of tribesmen led by their religious leader, the Mahdi.

Gordon could have escaped but did not and the city was under constant attack as the government in Britain dithered over whether a relieving force should be sent or not, some disapproving of the 'empire' aspect of the British presence, others pointing to Gordon's successes in stamping out slavery and giving the Sudan stable rule. Eventually, a relieving army was sent. It arrived two days

Young Lochinvar vaulted into the saddle, helped the bride up behind him, and was off!

after Gordon was slain when the city was sacked by the Mahdi's army.

If you are in the north-east go and visit magnificent Haddo House, once the home of Lord and Lady Aberdeen, and now in the care of the National Trust for Scotland.

It was there that Lord and Lady Aberdeen organised a 19th century social and dramatic club which drew its membership from all who lived at Haddo, including servants. Queen Victoria and high society were scandalised at such a breach of social barriers and conventions and the Queen ordered the prime minister to officially investigate the matter.

The minutes-book of this club gave playwright J.M.Barrie the idea for his play "The Admirable Crichton", in which the butler becomes the leader of a band of stranded, titled people on a desert island.

(The Gaelic name of the clan is **Clann Ghordan** and its war cry or slogan was "A Gordon, a Gordon!")

CLAN GRAHAM

Motto - "Ne oublie" ("Do not forget"- Montrose)
("Right and Reason"- Menteith)

Plant Badge - Laurel.

Territory - Several separate areas including the barony of Mugdock, north of Glasgow - parts of Menteith; around Loch Katrine in the Trossachs and close to Callander, around Loch Ard and Loch Venachar and the upper reaches of the Forth - the land around Kincardine Castle, Perthshire - around Dundee and at Old Montrose (close to the town of that name).

Sept names - Allardice, Bontein, Bontine, Bunten, Graeme, MacGilvernock, MacGrime, Monteith, Doig (Menteith).

The name Graham rings like a trumpet call in the pageant of Scottish history, and their allegiance to the royal house of Scotland has given them a reputation for loyalty that has stood the test of time (and despite the fact that one of them slew James I at the Blackfriars, Perth, in 1437).

There is perhaps not too much validity, however, in the story that a Graham (Gramus) first breached the Antonine Wall, the northern fixed defences of the Romans between the Forth and the Clyde, although it is true that part of the Wall is known as Graeme's Dyke.

The Grahams were probably Norman in origin, but quickly became aggressively Scottish. They fought staunchly for both Wallace and Bruce in the 14th century Scottish Wars of Independence, the 2nd Earl of Montrose was a friend of Cardinal Beaton at the time of the Reformation

The First Marquis of Montrose

and was loyal to Mary Queen of Scots and the third earl was a Protestant reformer and ended up Lord Chancellor and Viceroy. They were Earls of Menteith for nine centuries. But it is The Great Montrose and Bonnie Dundee who are the best known of the clan.

Montrose, as he is popularly known, was the fifth Earl and first Marquis of Montrose.

In the 17th century religious/political struggles, he initially supported the Covenant but became disillusioned and eventually set out to win Scotland for Charles I.

He was appointed Lieutenant-General in Scotland, travelled there in disguise, and raised the royal standard in 1644 at Blair Atholl.

Along with the great war leader of Clan Donald, Sir Alasdair MacDonald, known as Colkitto, he welded together Colkitto's 1,200 Irishmen and 3,000 Highland clansmen who were on the point of coming to blows and made them into a skilled and hardy army.

In a year - which became known as the year of miracles - they overwhelmingly defeated every army sent against them and won at least five major battles against great odds.

He held Scotland for a time but the final victory was not to be his. His forces split up and in September 1645 he was overwhelmed at Philiphaugh in the Scottish borders.

He tried again in 1650, was again defeated, and was finally handed over to the Marquis of Argyll's Covenanting forces by MacLeod of Assynt who had taken him prisoner.

His enemy, Argyll, had him hanged like a common criminal at the Grassmarket in Edinburgh the same year - his remains were later interred in St. Giles Cathedral, Edinburgh.

Like many another Scottish saga which has persevered it is a tale of heroic defeat against immense odds.

Montrose's famous verse is often quoted -
"He either fears his fate too much
Or his deserts are small,
Who dares not put it to the touch,
To win or lose it all".

In Scottish folk-memory, Montrose ranks with Wallace, Bruce and Bonnie Prince Charlie.

"Bonnie Dundee", as Sir Walter Scott's rousing song has it, was John Graham of Claverhouse, created Viscount Dundee.

He was born in 1649, a staunch Jacobite and he

persecuted the Covenanters to whom he was "Bluidy Clavers". Some said his black horse had been given to him by the Devil and that he was immune to bullets.

In 1688 he was second in command of the Scottish army and was ordered south to protect the Stewart throne when William of Orange was invited to be King in place of James VII (James II of England) who fled to France. Claverhouse came back to Scotland to raise the Clans in the Stuart cause.

In a carefully planned battle at Killiecrankie, in 1689, the fierce charge of the Jacobite clans swept the forces of King William, led by General Hugh MacKay, from the field and many were trapped and slain in the steep gorge of the Pass of Killiecrankie.

But Claverhouse was mortally wounded in the moment of victory.

As he was carried from the field he asked a Clansman: "How goes the day?" "Well for King James", said the man, "but I am sorry for your lordship".

"If it goes well for him", said Dundee, "it matters less for me".

But without his spirited leadership the Jacobite impetus was lost and the cause eventually petered out.

There were other Graham heroes as well, of course, and it was the third Duke of Montrose who, as Marquess of Graham, M.P., secured the repeal of the ban on tartan and the Highland dress brought in after the 1745 Jacobite Rising gave the Hanoverian government such a fright.

Weddings and christenings are normally times of joy and harmony but the Grahams were involved in two such occasions when blood was shed.

Some Stewarts of Appin were on their way home after a war campaign when they stopped at the house of the Earl of Menteith to ask for food. The earl and many of his men were away from home, hunting, but the servants were busy roasting chickens for a wedding feast. The Stewarts helped themselves and continued on their way.

The returning earl was furious, gathered together as many men as he could, and set off in hot pursuit.

He caught up with the Stewarts and a fierce fight broke out in which the earl, many of his men and most of the Stewarts were slain or mortally wounded.

The name "Grahams of the Hens" stuck from that day on as some Highland onlookers thought it an enormous to-do over a few roast chickens. But pride was at stake.

Another fracas broke out when Graham of Duchray was having his infant son baptised and the Graham, Earl of Airth, used this chance to try and arrest him for alleged misdeeds.

The Earl laid an ambush on Duchray's route to church and Duchray was stopped as he was crossing a bridge carrying the baby.

But Duchray was not easily cowed. He put the baby on the ground, drew sword and pistol, and said that as many as possible would drown in the river or die on that spot before he would surrender.

The male members of his baptism party also drew their swords and a full-scale confrontation was about to take place when the minister arrived and frantically persuaded both sides to have a truce.

Even at that, one of the earl's men had two fingers cut off and another was seriously wounded. Later, and after the baptism, an uneasy peace of a kind was agreed. Duchray got his freedom but undertook to behave himself.

CLAN GRANT

Motto - "Stand Fast".

Plant Badge - Pine and Cranberry

Territory - Strathspey, between two Craigellachies, at Aviemore and where the river Spey enters the Moray coastal plain, and the district of Rothiemurchas - the straths of Glen Urquhart and Glen Moriston, Loch Ness.

Sept names - Alanach, Gilroy, Kearns, Kerrons, MacGilroy, MacIlroy, MacKerron, MacKiaran, Patrick.

The Grants were excellent people at looking after themselves, administered their lands effectively and contracted some advantageous marriages.

The clan, as a whole, did not support the Stuart cause. During the 1715 Jacobite Rising, Glen Moriston fought for the Stuarts while other sections of the clan helped put the Rising down, and they did not officially 'come out' for Bonnie Prince Charlie in the '45 although Glen Moriston clansmen did so.

Some historians give the Grants a Norman origin but the Clan claims descent from Alpin who was reigning in Scotland more than two hundred years before William the Conqueror set foot in England.

They may have derived from MacGregor stock and when the MacGregors were being hounded and persecuted by some Scottisn monarchs and by powerful enemies the Grants gave them shelter and turned a blind eye to their presence.

They are a clan besprinkled with courageous men -one John Grant, offered a peerage by James VI, briskly asked - "And who'll be Laird o' Grant?"

Patrick Grant of Crasky was one of the Seven Men of Glen Moriston who guarded Bonnie Prnce Charlie during his wanderings as a fugitive, contemptuously rejecting the huge reward for the Prince's capture.

A champion boatman, Alistair Mor, when he was 18, obeyed a command of his chief to walk from Cromdale to London with his wicker-and-skin boat on his back to compete with champion scullers and rowers on the Thames.

His tiny craft skimmed the surface, leaving heavier boats far behind, and the London crowd warmed to the lad who won every contest.

Showered with gold pieces, he then presented them to his chief, commenting that he might care to buy some jewellery for Lady Grant.

A Grant piper once accepted a bet that he would walk from Inverness and then walk three times round Castle Grant continuously playing his pipes. The distance was 25 miles, the day was very hot, and the piper was close to exhaustion when he reached the castle.

He staggered round the castle on the first circuit, was almost on his knees for the second, the tune became more and more gaspingly unrecognisable on the third.

The crowd cheered him on and within a few yards of the final circuit the piper made a last great effort.

Patrick Grant protected the fugitive Prince Charlie and spurned offers of a reward.

The tune flared up for a few seconds and then ended in a long wail as the piper pitched forward on his face.

He was dead, 20 feet short of his goal.

A less attractive character was a fellow from Rothiemurchas known as Black Sandy.

He knew that a Grant laird was getting increasingly concerned because the laird's son had become attracted to his housekeeper and the housekeeper had borne the son three illegitimate children.

The laird didn't want the estate eventually divided up among such offspring so Black Sandy decided to give him a helping hand by ending the affair. His solution was drastic and grisly. He mutilated the housekeeper.

There was immense revulsion in the Clan over such an act and Black Sandy was forced to flee abroad.

He ended up in the United States and tradition has it that his great-grandson became General Ulysses Grant and President of the United States.

My sister, now resident in Canada, told me the following anecdote about the Grant slogan "Stand Fast Craigellachie".

A cairn in Eagle Pass, British Columbia, near the Alberta border, marks the spot where Donald Smith, a Canadian Pacific Railway director (representing his cousin, George Stephen, the company director) drove the last spike in the railway's trans-continental line on November 7, 1885.

A plaque beside the Trans-Canada Highway nearby records thet "a nebulous dream was a reality - an iron ribbon crossed Canada from sea to sea".

As the workers, foremen and bosses gathered for official photographs, the vice-president, Van Horne, suggested the spot be named Craigellachie, "the rallying place in Scotland of the Grant clan" from which both George Stephen and Donald Smith were descended. Modern Canadians, alas, pronounce it "Craigilatchie".

When the Canadian Pacific Railway project was desperately in need of funds Lord Mount Stephen, a partner in the scheme, sent a cable from London to fellow-partner Lord Strathcona, then High Commissioner for Canada, to let him know he had raised sufficient money to save the scheme. He used a pre-arranged code-word for success, the Grants war-slogan "Stand Fast, Craigellachie" (both men had Grant connections). Who said Clan links were a thing of the past?

CLAN MACGREGOR

Motto - **"S rioghal mo dhream"** ("My race is royal").

Plant Badge - Pine

Territory - Originally, Glen Orchy, Glen Strae, Glen Lochy (Argyll); latterly, Glen Lyon: Glendochart: parts of Rannoch: Balquhidder: Loch Lomondside, Loch Katrine-side and the Trossachs.

Septs - Gregor, Gregorson, Gregory, Greig, Grigor, Caird, Comrie, Crowther, Dochart, Fletcher, Grierson, King, Leckie, MacAdam, Macaree, Maconachie, MacNee, MacGruder, MacNeish, Malloch, Peter, Petrie, White, Whyte.

The MacGregors claim descent from one of Scotland's early Kings, Kenneth Alpin, hence the wording of their motto.

They were a tough and tenacious Clan and endured great persecution by powerful enemies or Scottish monarchs who were exasperated by their prowess in war and their understandable belligerance and tendency to answer insult with insult (or worse).

Sir Walter Scott called them the Children of the Mist but the various proscriptions against them at various times were very ugly; their very name was banned, they were forbidden weapons, to gather in numbers, could be killed on sight, a bounty was paid for their heads, their womenfolk could be branded, their children taken away and given to other clans or families to bring up, their homes burned, and their lands arbitrarily seized.

Many temporarily took other names or went underground and it is only fair to say that some clans gave them succour and shelter. They survived all hardships and, as Sir Walter wrote in his famous song, "The MacGregors Gathering": "MacGregor, despite them, shall flourish for ever".

They were squeezed from their Argyllshire lands by the Campbells and moved westwards and, considering that they had themselves moved into the lands of others, they settled down tolerably well although, to central authority, they were technically landless.

Grave punishment fell upon them in the 16th century following one of these minor incidents that sometimes spill over into major wars.

Two MacGregors travelling through Colquhoun country on the shores of Loch Lomond were refused food at a Colquhoun house, a rare occurrence in the hospitable Highlands. They then killed, cooked and ate a sheep. They were found by the Colquhouns in a ruined barn the next day with the sheep's skin beside them. Offers to pay went unheeded and the Colquhouns hanged them both.

The rest of the MacGregor Clan were enraged at the news and a fullscale feud developed.

Some of the MacGregors attacked the Colquhouns of Luss and there were several dead.

A procession of Colquhoun widows travelled to Stirling carrying their husbands' bloodstained shirts on the points of lances.

James VI was horrified and he gave the Colquhouns royal authority to be an official (if somewhat one-sided) peace-keeping force in the area and to put the MacGregors down.

But the MacGregors had other ideas and on February 7, 1603, they ambushed and outfought a combined army of Colquhouns and Buchanans in Glen Fruin.

They also slew citizens of the town of Dumbarton who had either come out to see the fun or who were part of the Colquhoun army (it depends on which clan historian you favour).

James VI was furious and ordered dire punishment for the MacGregors. Alastair MacGregor and 11 of his chieftains were eventually hanged at the Mercat Cross in Edinburgh on January 20, 1604.

As an honorary member of the Clan Gregor Association, I must point out that the MacGregors state the quarrel was not of their making, they were not permitted to refute the Colquhoun widows' complaint which they regarded as a piece of stage management, and the Glen Fruin affair was a justified instance of the better side winning.

Yet, in later centuries, the MacGregors fought for the Stuart cause, partly in the hope that the Stuarts, if successful, would give them their lands back and partly because many of their enemies supported William of Orange or the Hanoverians, and also to defend the values of Highland Gaeldom.

One of the Seven Men of Glen Moriston, who sheltered the fugitive Bonnie Prince Charlie, was a MacGregor.

The Clan's best known son is almost certainly Rob Roy MacGregor, born in 1671, in Glen Gyle, Loch Katrine, who became tutor to the young chief and de facto leader of a branch of the Clan.

Erroneously called the Scottish Robin Hood (he is entirely factual) he fought for the Jacobites when lesser men stayed at home, and eventually built up a large cattle business.

He was ruined when his assistant absconded with his funds and his enemies seized the opportunity to seize his lands and persecute him.

He smote them mightily, defended the poor and oppressed against the rich and powerful, and successfully outwitted two dukes and the Army. Tales of him became legend and Daniel Defoe wrote a pamphlet about him, King George I expressed an admiration for him and Sir Walter Scott wrote a novel about him but the truth is greater than the legend. He died, surprisingly, in his bed and was buried in Balquhidder churchyard in 1734. Read W.H.Murray's definitive biography "Rob Roy Macgregor: His Life and Times" (Richard Drew, Glasgow); it is a marvellous portrait of the man and his age.

The Macgregor's war-cry or slogan is **"Ard Choille"** ("The High Wood") and their Gaelic name **Clann Ghriogair.**

ROB ROY MACGREGOR

The following story has also been ascribed to the MacDonalds of Glen Coe but is generally told of the MacGregors and it was certainly the MacGregors who gathered in Balquhidder Church for their grisly oath.

It all had its origins in the high affairs of state when James VI in October 1589 was going to Oslo (in what is now Norway) to bring home the Danish Princess Anne whom he had married by proxy.

Venison naturally was to figure on the menus of many a feast and Lord Patrick Drummond of Perth, Steward of Strathearn and the Chief Forester of the Royal Forest of Glen Artney, was instructed to see to supplies and he, in turn, got his chief forester John Drummond-Ernoch (or Eireannach) to organise it.

Drummond-Ernoch, on his legal business, caught some men poaching deer and cut their ears off.

Some traditions say they were MacDonalds but written accounts say they were MacGregors.

In any event, a band of MacGregors came to Glen Artney, caught Drummond-Ernoch, and cut his head off.

His sister (some stories say it was his daughter) was married to Stewart of Ardvorlich, on the south shore of Loch Earn, and they took themselves off there and, in the Highland tradition of hospitality, asked for food.

She gave them bread and cheese and then left the room to get something more substantial.

When she returned the dripping head of her brother was on the table.

She was pregnant and rushed shrieking from the house up into Glen Vorlich, where there were shieling huts.

The late Dr. Seton Gordon, that marvellous naturalist, mountaineer and historian, said she sheltered high up in the hills above Glen Vorlich and that a lochan, not named on modern maps, Lochan na Mna, the small loch-of-the-woman, commerorates this event.

She was deranged for some days but was eventually persuaded to return home, and had her baby.

The baby, James Stewart, grew up into a moody youth of violent temper and he eventually became a staff officer in Montrose's army, during the 17th century Wars of the Covenant, and murdered Lord Kilpont in an obscure and puzzling camp brawl.

The MacGregors left Ardvorlich Castle with the gruesome head and took themselves off to Balquhidder

Church. At the Kirkton end of Loch Voil on a piece of land still called Inch MacGregor or Macgregor's Isle, lived the Macgregor chief's brother, Ian Dubh.

(Incidentally, if you want to read a splendid book about Balquhidder get hold of Elizabeth Beauchamp's "The Braes o' Balquhidder" (Heatherbank Press, Milngavie, Glasgow).

The chief, Alasdair MacGregor of Glen Strae, was sent for and a macabre ceremony took place in the little church, the **Eaglais-beag** (not the present church, but on that site.)

The head of Drummond Ernoch was put on the altar and the chief placed his hand on it and promised to protect the killers.

The whole clan followed on and did the same, all-for-one and one-for-all.

It is understandable that the hounded MacGregors realised that only in the most closely-knit support for one another could they survive, but immense retribution was to fall on them.

Twelve leading Highland nobles or chiefs were ordered to capture the chief and his brother and 135 named members of the clan, and some were indeed caught and hanged.

Others survived and fought back but there were to be many bloody and dangerous days ahead.

CLAN MACKAY

Motto · Manu forti ("With a strong hand").

Plant Badge · Great Bulrush, reed grass.

Territory · Strathnaver to the northern coast, westwards to the coast, eastwards to Strath Halladale, southwards to the lovely bay of Eddrachillis with its many islets, and to Forsinard.

Sept names · Bain, Bayne, MacBain, MacCay, MacCrie, Mackee, Mackie, MacPhail (Sutherland), MacQuay, MacQuoid, Neilson, Polson, Reay, Scobie, MacGee, MacGhie, Morgan, Paul, Williamson.

You've got to hand it to the Mackays, they could certainly look after themselves. They had a deserved reputation for staunchness and the American expression, the "Real MacCoy", a guarantee of true worthiness, is thought to derive from the name of migrants. In its Scottish origin, of course, the real MacKay, was used to distinguish between the over-all chief and junior claimants.

The clan may have had Norse origins and their turbulence got them expelled from Moray and Clan Morgan, as a main branch was then known, went north and settled in Strath Naver, that lovely wide glen later to be notorious as one of the worst areas affected by the 19th century Highland Clearances.

Like the MacGregors they frequently held no land charter and operated by the prowess of their swords.

One of the offspring of Clan Morgan was called Aodh (pronounced Iye) and from him came the name MacAodh or Mackay. James I had trouble with the clan chiefs and he invited about 40 to meet him in Inverness for full, frank and friendly discussions in an atmosphere of mutual esteem, as we say in industrial negotiations nowadays.

But he jailed the most unruly, as he saw it.

Among them was Angus Dubh (Black Angus), known as Angus the Absolute and he could put 4,000 men into the field. Poor Angus was forced to surrender his son Neil as hostage and Neil, who must have felt very aggrieved, was kept prisoner on the Bass Rock for ten years.

were tough. Angus sent for his youngest son, Iain Aberach (Abrach), then staying with kinspeople in Lochaber, and he hurried home on foot, no mean journey.

On arrival he asked for food and was directed to the door of the dining hall only to find it blocked by a fierce boarhound. The dog leaped at his throat but, tired and hungry though he was, he whipped out his dirk and slew it. Panting and angry, he was embraced by his father who expressed his delight at the test of courage of a son he had not seen for years.

He said "Dearbh thu do cridhe" ("you have proved your valour!"). And that is now the motto, or war-slogan, of the cadet Aberach (Abrach) family. Another Mackay motto is "Bi treum!" ("Be valiant").

Angus saw his son lead the Mackays to victory over the Earl of Sutherland's army at Drumnacoub, near Tongue, but was himself killed by an arrow when, too frail to bear arms himself, he was tending the wounded. Ah well, as the Gaelic proverb has it, better a swift death on the battlefield than a slow one in bed. Before the battle the Sutherlands had taunted the Mackays over the youth of their leader: "We will put a hobble on yonder calf". But the Mackays had the last laugh.

The Mackay-Sutherland feud then grew bitter and, alas, the Mackays chased their enemies into the chapel of St. Duthus (Duthuc) at Tain and killed them, setting fire to the building. Central authority felt this was a bit much and the leading culprit was apprehended and executed.

The Mackays swung their swords overseas as well. Charles I raised Donald, the chief, to the peerage as Lord Reay and he raised a brigade of merceneries.

Iain whipped out his dirk and slew the fierce boarhound.

They fought for the King of Denmark and they also have a permanent place in European history by their exploits in serving under the famous Gustavus Adolphus of Sweden, "The Lion of the North", on behalf of the Protestant cause in the Thirty Years War. The respect for them and which they, in turn, gave to their leader, is seen in the fact that many Mackay babies were given the name Gustavus.

One of the most famous Mackays, General Hugh Mackay, of Scourie, was so successful as a military commander that monarchs competed for his services. He served William of Orange in the Netherlands and so began the Mackay's Dutch connection. One branch of the family settled there and was granted a title and land. The family produced a prime minister of the Netherlands.

General Mackay's Scottish clashes were not so memorable. He commanded the army routed by John Graham of Claverhouse, "Bonnie Dundee", at Killiecrankie in 1689 and is referred to in a song, with words adapted by Robert Burns, which is sung to this day.

The Mackay land was very fertile, broad straths, good rivers, sea-fishing and arable land at the coast so it is not surprising they could supply many warriors.

Their Gaelic name is **Clann Mhich Mhorgain** or **Clann Aoidh.** Their war cry is "Bratach ban Mhic Aoidh!" ("The white banner of Mackay"). This legendary banner can still be seen in the National Museum of Antiquities in Edinburgh.

CLAN MACKENZIE

Motto - "Luceo non uro" ("I shine, not burn").

Plant Badge - Deer's grass, holly.

Territory - Originally Kintail: then expansion until at one stage the Mackenzie lands spread from Applecross and the west right across Scotland to the Moray Firth, covering most of the old county of Ross and Cromarty, and including Strathconan and Strathgarve (west of Dingwall), Strathpeffer and Beauly, part of the Black Isle, and part of Lewis in the Outer Hebrides.

Sept names - Charleson, Kenneth, Kennethson, MacConnach, MacBeolain, MacKerlich, MacVanish, MacVinish, Murchie, Murchieson. The Mathesons, MacLennans and MacRaes, although separate clans, had a historic attachment to the Mackenzies. The MacRaes held spectacular Eilean Donan castle, in Kintail, and were known as "Mackenzie's Shirt of Mail".

The Clan name derives from the Gaelic **Mac Coinnich** (MacKenneth, son of Kenneth), anglicised as Mackenzie. Their war slogan is "Tulloch Ard" ("The High Hill").
We rightly honour the men whose names, and far too many of them, appear on the war memorials because they died that we might live in freedom and, in a very real sense, they are the successors of the brave, warrior tradition of the clans. There is no greater love, runs the old saying, than that a man lay down his life for his friends.
We should, therefore, honour Roderick Mackenzie. He was a personal guard to Prince Charles Edward Stuart,

80

Bonnie Prince Charlie, and he was also similar to the Prince in build and appearance.

When the Prince was a fugitive after the battle of Culloden in 1746 Roderick Mackenzie was surprised and overcome by some of Cumberland's soldiers. He resisted them and was struck down at a spot close to the Prince's hiding place in Glen Moriston. He knew nothing could save his own life but he was determined to save the Prince. As he fell, he shouted: "You have killed your Prince! You have killed your Prince!".

The soldiers were elated because they thought they could claim the £30,000 reward for the Prince's capture, an enormous sum by today's prices. The Duke of Cumberland, commanding the Hanoverian forces in Scotland, was delighted with the news and urgent steps were taken to have Roderick's head positively identified.

In the meanwhile, the hunt for the Prince slackened and this eanbled him and his friends to slip away and seek further refuge with the MacPhersons in Badenoch. The mistake was discovered, but too late. The bird had flown.

A cairn of remembrance was later erected to Roderick's memory in Glen Moriston.

The Mackenzies were great fighters and in the 18th century their descendants formed the regiment, the Seaforth Highlanders, now part of the Queen's Own Highlanders. The chief's crest is a stag's head and it is the product of an old story.

King Alexander III, who reigned in the 13th century, was hunting in the Forest of Mar with many of the leading Clan chiefs when his life was in peril. In the days before firearms, deer were chased by hounds and cornered in 'folds' (called **elrigs** in Gaelic), stone-walls in the shape of a pen, where they were slain by axe, spear, sword and arrow. Sometimes cornered deer rounded on their hunters and maimed or even killed them.

The king saw a stag with fine antlers and it was driven towards him. Suddenly, it charged at him.

Instantly, Kenneth of Kintail, the chief, shouted in Gaelic "Cuidich an Righ!" ("Save the King!"). He quickly shot an arrow, a risky thing to do because the King was in his line of fire. But his aim was precise. The stag was brought down.

The King was saved. In gratitude the King awarded the Mackenzies a stag's head as the family's armorial bearings and the motto "Cuidich an Righ". The Seaforths

Kenneth's aim was precise and the stag was brought down.

regiment later adopted this crest and motto as their own.

The ninth chief of Kintail, John was a clever man who, unlike some other chiefs, was adept at holding and acquiring land by charters although he could also call out his Clansmen with great effectiveness.

He was taken prisoner at the great Scottish disaster at Flodden in 1513, but was freed by an almost unbelievable coincidence. His English escort stopped for the night at a house where there lived a woman who had once been shipwrecked and sheltered in the Mackenzie country. She aided his escape.

Highland pride could sometimes be upstaged by a realistc sense of the practical. A tale goes that Mary Queen of Scots sent her chamberlain and other officials to assess the wealth of the Highland chiefs so that they could be taxed. When they visited John he arranged for his men to scatter dung and offal, old skins and soiled straw around the house so the visitors quickly left. They reported he was a poor man and he benefited accordingly when the royal taxes were ordered.

One of the strangest Mackenzies was Kenneth Mackenzie, **Coinnich Odhar**, the Brahan Seer, who had the gifts of prophecy and second-sight. He was born at Baile-na-Chille, Uig, on the island of Lewis, early in the 17th century. He had a sarcastic tongue and the wife of the 3rd Earl of Seaforth became so resentful towards him she had him accused of witchcraft and burned to death. The Seer made a dire prophecy.

He read the doom of the race of his oppressor. The long-descended line of Seaforth would, before many generations had passed, end in sorrow. He saw a chief, the last of his house, who was deaf and dumb. This chief would have four sons, all of whom he would follow to the grave. He would live careworn and die mourning, knowing that no future chief of the MacKenzies should bear rule at Brahan or in Kintail. After lamenting the last and most promising of his sons he would himself die. The remnants of his possessions would be inherited by a white-coiffed (a close fitting cap) girl from the east who would kill her own sister. As a sign that this would happen, he said, there would be four great lairds in the days of this last Seaforth, of whom one would be buck-toothed, another hare-lipped, another half-witted and the fourth a stammerer. These men would be his friends and allies: each time he looked at them he would know his sons would die, his lands pass to strangers and his race would end.

A century later it became true. Francis Humberstone MacKenzie, last Earl of Seaforth, fell ill with scarlet fever when a boy and became deaf. He married and had four sons. Among his friends were MacKenzie of Gairloch, who was buck-toothed, Chisholm of Chisholm who had a hare-lip, Grant of Grant who was mentally defective and MacLeod of Raasay who had a stutter. He suffered financial losses from his estates in the West Indies and had to sell much of his Highland land. Then three of his four sons died. Later the fourth died when a teenager and Seaforth himself, stricken by grief, went to his grave. Two sections of the prophecy were still outstanding - the white-coiffed girl and the killing of her sister. This, too, came to pass.

Seaforth's eldest daughter, who lived in the East Indies wore a white coiff when she came home to inherit the property because her husband, Sir Samuel Hood, had died and she was otherwise wearing widow's black. One day she took her younger sister, the Hon. Caroline MacKenzie, out for a drive in a pony carriage and when they passed close to the spot where the Brahan Seer had lived the two ponies took fright and bolted. Both girls were thrown out. The injuries of the elder girl (who had worn the white coiff) were slight but the younger girl was killed.

So ended the dreadful prophecy. The Seer made many others and they make intriguing reading.

(The Brahan Seer is a controversial subject. Some authorities say he is a shadowy figure, others that his prophecies were made by other seers, but the tale and the tradition persist).

CLAN MACLEAN

This great clan had four main branches, Duart, Maclaine of Lochbuie, MacLean of Ardgour and of Coll.

Motto - "Altera Merces" ("Reward is Secondary"), Duart. "Vincere vel mori" ("Victory or death"), Lochbuie.

Plant Badge - Crowberry (Duart), Blueberry (Lochbuie), Holly (Ardgour and Coll).

Territory - Mull, Tiree, Coll, parts of Islay and Jura, Scarba, Luing, Morven, Ardgour, Knapdale, the west coast almost to Glenfinnan: a northern branch had lands at Glen Urquhart, on the north shore of Loch Ness.

Sept names - Bethune, Beton, Black, MacBeath, MacBeth, MacVeagh, Garvie, Gillan, Gilzean, Lean, Macilduy (all Duart): MacCormick, MacFadyen, MacPhadden, Patten, MacFadzean (all Lochbuie), Gribban (northern MacLeans), and other names include MacLergain, MacRankin and Rankin.

The MacLeans lived in some of the most lovely areas of the West Highlands. They were great seamen who could command many galleys. They were also staunch adherents of the Stuart dynasty and suffered accordingly.

Of 180 MacLeans who were 'out' with the Jacobites in the 1745 Rising only about 38 returned home. They were prominent in many campaigns over the centuries.

They claim descent from **Gilleathain na Tuaighe,** Gillian of the Battleaxe, who fought fiercely against the Norsemen at the battle of Largs in 1263 when the Scots broke the Norse bid to hold Scotland's western seaboard.

An old legend says that Gillian was hunting deer on Mull when he lost his way in thick mist. Ultimately, he felt so exhausted that he lay down to die but he hung his axe on the branch of a laurel to mark his last resting place under a cypress bush. It's a bit of a puzzle why such a hardy man on his own ground should be lost for so long but there it is. Searchers saw the axe and then found him. He later recovered. The axe, the laurel and the cypress are now all in the MacLean coat of arms.

Although it was the encroaching and expansionist Campbells the MacLeans were wary of, they also clashed with the MacDonalds and they had a dispute over lands on Islay. Sir Lachlan Mor MacLean (Lachlan the Great), 14th chief of Duart, is said to have consulted a witch about what he should do and the witch advised that he not land on Islay on a Thursday and *not* drink from a well called "Strange Neil's Well". But storms forced him ashore on Islay and, unknowingly, he drank from the haunted spring. Retribution fell on him.

Before the battle a dwarf from Jura ,known as "Dubh Sith" ("Black Elf") offered Sir Lachlan his help but was contemptuously brushed aside. Enraged at the slight, the Dubh Sith offered his help to the MacDonalds. He climbed a tree and when he got within arrow range of Sir Lachlan he noted an open joint in his armour and put an arrow right through the slit. It was known as the battle of the Rhinns of Islay.

Sometimes, too, the MacLean branches differed among themselves and after a fierce clash over a land quarrel the Lochbuie MacLeans defeated the Duart MacLeans. But when the victorious Lochbuie chief was on his way home he found Duart and some of his men sound asleep, exhausted after the hard fight. He drew his dirk and carefully pinned his rival's hair to the ground.

When Duart awoke he recognised the dirk and realised his opponent had refrained from killing him. He was touched by the chivalry of the act and the families ended the feud and stayed friends and allies from then on.

Not so attractive a story is the tale of Lachlan MacLean of Duart who married Elizabeth, a sister of the Earl of Argyll. Their marriage was not happy and he decided to get rid of her. He had her bound and then marooned at low tide on a prominent rock in the sea between the lovely island of Lismore and Mull. The next day she had

Elizabeth was bound and marooned at low tide on a prominent rock in the sea by her scheming husband.

gone. He sent a mesage of a drowning tragedy to her kinsfolk at Inveraray, the Campbell capital. He travelled there to pay his condolences and much to his consternation he found her sitting in a room flanked by her relatives. A passing fishing boat had rescued her.

Surprisingly, the Campbells let him go instead of killing him out of hand. Perhaps they believed in the Italian proverb that revenge is a dish that should be eaten cold. A year later, when he was in Edinburgh, he was stabbed to death by Campbell of Cawdor.

If you are ever on the island of Kerrera, near Oban, or Lismore, or going by boat to Mull, you can see Lady's Rock for yourself.

The MacLeans were noted for their bravery. When Red Hector, the 18th chief, was at Inverkeithing in battle against the Cromwellian army he found himself surrounded. His own men saw that the enemy were trying to take him prisoner, or kill him, and they shielded him in the thick of the fight. Seven men gave their lives in his defence and as each fell another stepped into his place shouting **"Fear eile airson Eachainn!"** ("Another for Hector!"), and this shout became a Clan war-slogan.

If you go to Mull you can visit Duart Castle on its prominent rock. It was a ruin for 220 years and then Sir Fitzroy Donald MacLean, the 26th chief, began its restoration in 1912. It is now very much as it was. MacLeans are tough. Sir Fitzroy Donald MacLean died in 1937 when he was 102.

The Gaelic name of the Clan is **Clann Gilleathain.** In addition to "Another For Hector" another war-cry is "Beatha no Bas!" ("Life or Death").

CLAN MACLEOD

Mottoes - "Hold Fast!" (MacLeod of Harris), "Luceo non uro", (I shine, not burn), (MacLeod of Lewis).

Plant Badges - Juniper (Harris), Red whortleberry (Lewis).

Territory - In Skye (at various times) Duirinish, Bracadale, Minginish, Dunvegan, Sleat, Trotternish, Waternish and Snizort: Harris, North Uist; Glen Elg; part of Lewis; Soay; Raasay; Assynt; Coigach peninsula and Gairloch.

Sept names - Beaton, Bethune, Beton, Harold, MacCaig, MacLure, MacCuag, MacLure, MacRaild, Malcolmson, Norman (all Harris): Callum (Raasay): Lewis, MacAskill, MacCorkindale, MacNicol, Nicholson (Lewis).

The Clan MacLeod would go down well in Spain as they seemed to be able to take on fierce bulls and win.

In the 14th century Malcolm MacLeod of Glen Elg was said to be in love with Fraser of Glen Elg's wife and when he was returning home from a secret meeting he was met and confronted by a savage bull.

He killed it, reputedly by breaking its neck, and in the struggle one of its horns broke off. The horn was later made into a drinking cup tipped with silver and became known as the drinking cup of Rory Mor, after a famous MacLeod chief. When the MacLeod chief comes of age he is expected to drain it.

Long ago one of the MacLeod chiefs of Dunvegan went to Inveraray to visit the Earl of Argyll and when he was there he was invited to attend the execution of a Campbell who had misbehaved and who was to be gored to death by a bull.

When the man was led into the arena he showed such calm courage thet the MacLeod pleaded for his release. Argyll said it was not possible and nothing, at that stage, could save the man.

MacLeod seized one of the horns with his hand and
clung on as he was tossed about.

MacLeod asked if he could have him if he saved him and prepared to leap into the pit. Argyll reluctantly agreed but added: "You go to your death". MacLeod leaped down and as the bull lowered its head for the charge he seized one of the horns and clung on as he was tossed about.

A spectator shouted: "Hold fast!".

He did so and managed to stab the bull with his dirk. And the bull's head and the motto "Hold Fast" are in the armorial bearings of the MacLeods of Harris to this day.

The three-legs of the Isle of Man armorial bearings are also used because the Clan is believed to be descended from a Viking ancestor, the son of Olaf the Black, King of Man. Leod married the heiress of Dunvegan who was the daughter of a Norwegian chief. They had two sons, Tormod who founded the MacLeods of Harris, Glen Elg and Dunvegan, and Torquil who founded the MacLeods of Lewis and Assynt. The Gaelic names are **Clann Tormod (Thormoid)** and **Clann Torquil (Thorcuil).**

Dunvegan Castle, on Skye, has been lovingly looked after and at 500 years it is the oldest continually inhabited house in Britain used by the same family who built it.

If you visit there you can see the Brattich Shithe, the famous Fairy Flag. A legend says a faery princess married a MacLeod and as she was summoned back to faeryland she dropped her cloak and that's the flag. Another tale says that when a MacLeod heir was born his nurse slipped away to watch or take part in the carousings. The bedclothes slipped off the new baby and faeries wrapped him in a silken flag. When the nurse returned she carried the baby into the great hall and mysterious voices said the flag had magic powers.

If produced in battle it would make an enemy believe that the MacLeods had more men than they actually had. It would ensure the succession of the family and it would bring herring into the loch (which meant prosperity). But it could only be waved three times and if a fourth were ever to take place the flag and bearer would disappear from the earth.

It was waved in 1490 at the Battle of Glendale when the MacLeods defeated the MacDonalds in a land quarrel and, thanks to the 19th century MacLeods who looked after their people in time of hunger and distress (when others were clearing the people from the land to make way for sheep), the Clan are still at Dunvegan. In modern

A MacLeod piper at Dunvegan.

times the late Dame Flora MacLeod did much to rekindle Clan links.

The flag is a mystery. It measures four feet by two and the silk was woven in either Syria or Rhodes and darns in it were made in the Near East. It may have been a holy relic originally. Harald Hardrada, from whom Leod, 1st chief, was descended, was in Constantinople in the 11th century, but there is no certainty about its origin. Perhaps the faeries should get the vote - it certainly works.

Occasionally all seemed lost for the MacLeods but they always seemed to recover.

At the disastrous battle of Worcester in 1651 the Siol Tormod were almost wiped out, losing over 700 men. By the consent of other chiefs they were excused later military service until they had recovered. They were so disgruntled by offhand treatment that they never again came out for the Stuart dynasty (other MacLeods, such as the MacLeods of Raasay, did join the Jacobite cause but not in full strength).

The MacCrimmons, the most famous family of Scottish pipers, are septs of the MacLeods and for centuries were hereditary pipers to the chiefs. They had a college at Borevaig, on Skye.

John Dubh MacCrimmon, last of his race to hold the hereditary post, decided to emigrate to America in 1795. Piping was in a bad way because the pipes, as well as tartan and weapons, were banned by the Hanoverian government for a period after the failure of the 1745 Jacobite Rising. He must have been a very reluctant migrant because when he reached his port of embarkation at Greenock his love for his own land overcame him and he returned to Skye. Perhaps it was the glorious scenery of the hills and water of the Firth of Clyde that so reminded him of Skye that his heart was caught. He died in Skye in 1822 aged 91.

CLAN ROBERTSON

Motto · "Virtutis gloria merces" ("Glory is the Reward of Valour").

Plant Badge · Bracken.

Territory · From Rannoch Moor eastwards, bounded on the north by Loch Rannoch and the south by Glen Lyon, and almost to Loch Tummell (22 miles), then north for 12 miles with Drumochter Pass and Loch Garry marking the western boundary and Bruar Water the east; another pocket lay south-east of the River Tilt and another on the south bank of the Tay between Grandtully and Dunkeld.

Sept names · Collier, Donachie, Duncan, Duncanson, Dunnachie, Inches, MacDonachie, Macinroy, MacLagan, MacRobie, MacRobert, Reid, Roy, MacConachie, MacRobb, Stark.

The Robertsons were never a large clan but they were amongst the most stalwart, loyal and courageous. They are also known as Clan Donnachie after a chief called **Donnachaidh Reamhar,** Duncan the Sturdy, and at times the Donnachies almost had a separate identity.

There is a Clan Donnachie museum at the Falls of Bruar on the A.9 between Perth and Inverness and it is well worth stopping there and having a look around.

The Clan's Gaelic name is **Clann Dhonnachaidh** and its war-slogan is **"Garg'n uair dhuisgear!"** (**"Fierce When Roused''**).

The Clan gave King Robert the Bruce great help in the 14th century Scottish Wars of Independence. When Duncan Reamhar brought his Clansmen to fight for Bruce at Bannockburn in 1314 the King is reputed to have said that up until then they had been called the sons of Duncan (a reference to another ancestor) but from then on they were to be called his children, hence Robert-son was used.

(The derivation might also be from Robert, the fourth chief, but it deserves to be a true story).

The modern Clan Society still prize one of the oldest Clan relics in Scotland. When they were on their way to Bannockburn they halted for the night and their standard bearer laid their flag beside him on the ground. When he lifted it the next day a precious stone, like a ball of milky crystal, was found sticking to it.

The Clan looked upon this as a good omen and they called it **Clach-nan- Brattich** or Stone of the Banner (or Ensign) and had it fixed to the top of their standard pole.

They were always great supporters of the Stuart monarchs. When King James I was murdered in Blackfriars Monastery in Perth in 1451 the chief, Robert **Riabhach** (Grizzled) hunted down and captured the killers. James II made Robert's lands into the Barony of Struan as a reward and a crest was added to the chief's coat of arms which showed a hand and arm holding up a royal crown with a man in chains hanging from the shield.

The fighting reputation of one of the most famous chiefs, Alexander, is remembered to this day. He fought in three Jacobite Risings. He joined Claverhouse in 1688 and eventually had to take temporary refuge in France after Claverhouse was killed at Killiecrankie and the rising fizzled out. In the 1715 he and 500 of his men were at the raising of the Jacobite Standard on the Braes of Mar and he fought at Sheriffmuir. He was twice taken prisoner and twice escaped and again got away safely to France.

He was 75 when the '45 came along but off he went again to fight for the Jacobites at the victorious battle of Prestonpans. When the army set off into England his younger leaders persuaded him to go home for a time. So he did it in style. He travelled in the captured coach of Sir John Cope, the Hanoverian commander, and when the tracks got too rough for the carriage wheels his tough clansmen simply carried it with their elderly chief sometimes walking alongside and sometimes sitting in-

The clansmen carried their elderly chief in style.

side in state. He was also a brilliant poet and scholar and his poems were published after his death in 1749.

If you like music, both military and classical, then you will like General John Reid, the son of Alexander Robertson of Straloch, whose ancestors were called **Rua,** roy or red, because the family had red hair. The general did not sign himself Robertson but kept the name and signature of 'red' which he changed to Reid. He was an expert flute player and a great lover of music. He became a major in the 42nd Regiment (The Black Watch) and he set the words of "The Garb of Old Gaul" to music and it became the regimental march.

He left a vast sum of money to establish a professorship at Edinburgh University where he had been a student. In his will he asked that on or about January 13, the date of his birthday, an annual concert should be held in the hall of the professor of music and the programme should begin with one of his own compositions and include "The Garb of Old Gaul".

The Reid concert tradition began and still continues and the audience still rise for "The Garb of Old Gaul".

(The garb of old Gaul is, of course, the kilt).

CLAN STEWART

Motto - "Virescit vulnere virtus" ("Courage grows strong at a wound"), Stewart, Royal.
"Quidder we'll zye" ("Whither will ye"),Stewart of Appin.

Plant Badge - The oak and the thistle.

Territory - Appin; Balquhidder; Bute and Arran: areas of Atholl including Grandtully, Garth Castle and Balnakeilly: areas around Loch Katrine, Loch Voil and Loch Earn including Ardvorlich: area south-east of Callander, including Doune Castle (the Earls of Moray): around Elgin (Darnaway Castle and Lochindorb Castle, the latter the operational base of the infamous Wolf of Badenoch, a younger brother of King Robert III, pillager, murderer and all-round "heid-case").

Sept names - Appin - Carmichael, Combich, Levack, Livingstone, MacCombich, MacKinlay, MacLay and MacMichael.
Atholl - Crookshanks, Cruickshanks, Duilach, Gray, McGlashan.
Bute - Bannatyne, Fullerton, Jameson, Jamieson, MacCamie, MacCaw, MacCloy, MacKirdy, MacLewis, MacMunn, MacMutrie,
Royal line septs - Boyd, France, Garrow, Lennox, Monteith.

It might seem odd at first sight that the Chancellor of the Exchequer and the Stewarts have a close connection but that's the truth of it.

Nearly every branch of the Stewart family has in their coat of arms or armorial bearings a sign that looks like a section of a chessboard, black and white squares or 'dices'. You can see a similar pattern on the peaked caps of Scottish policemen. It is a recognised heraldic device called 'the checky'.

Centuries ago accounting was done in squares like those on a chess board which were marked out on a board of cloth beside which, or around which, accountants or *stewards* sat.

Counters were used on the squares and they represented sums of money paid to or due by the treasurer of revenues. The High Stewardship of Scotland was made a hereditary appointment in the 12th century and the family of one Walter Fitz Alan took the device into their coat-of-arms. So, today, we still talk of the Exchequer and the Chancellor of the Exchequer, many centuries after the system was used.

The Stewarts trace their descent from Banquo, Thane of Lochaber, and through him the ancient kings of Scotland. Banquo was murdered by MacBeth, one of the best kings Scotland had and it must be pointed out that Shakespeare's magnificent play is highly innaccurate history.

Banquo's son, Fleance, escaped and fled to Wales where he fell in love with a princess and made his rivals so jealous that they killed him. But his son, Walter, fled overseas and took refuge at the court of Alan the Red of Brittany, in what is now France. In gratitude for the protection he received he took the name Fitz Alan (Fitz in Welsh is the same as 'Mac', son of, in Scotland).

When William the Conqueror invaded England Walter eventually made his way north to Scotland. He succeeded in so pleasing King David I that he made him his High Steward.

As the system of surnames evolved in Scotland Stewart became a settled form.

The family had many branches and cadet houses and produced five earls, Angus, Lennox, Menteith, Buchan, Traquair, as well as many other powerful leaders.

The sixth High Steward, also called Walter, gave great support to King Robert the Bruce in the 14th century Scottish Wars of Independence. He married Bruce's daughter, Marjorie, and their son became King Robert II, and the Royal line evolved from that.

Stuart instead of Stewart is a French form, a link with Scotland's ties with France and with Mary Queen of Scots in particular, but has come to be the accepted spelling for Royalty.

The story of the Stewarts is the story of Scots history because for centuries they were the leading dynasty. But it is the clan aspect we are mainly concerned with in this book and the Highland Stewarts had five main branches, Appin, Atholl, Balquhidder, the Earls of Moray and the Marquesses of Bute.

One of them, Duncan, the sixth chief of Appin, infuriated his fellow clansmen by getting drunk and handing over Castle Stalker (now beautifully restored), in Appin Bay, to Campbell of Airds in exchange for an eight-oared wherry (boat). He was, alas, held to his promises when he sobered up.

The Stewarts of Appin were great fighters. They joined Montrose and Colkitto MacDonald in the Scottish Wars of the Covenant, fought at Killiecrankie, and at Sheriffmuir, and were also out in the '45, suffering heavy casualties at Culloden. Nearly 100 of the Appin men fell in that last, gallant charge of the Clans and their flag, of pale blue with a yellow saltire, can be seen in Edinburgh Castle with the musket ball holes still in it. Brigadier Ian Stewart of Achnacone, Appin, once showed me the muster roll of the Stewarts of Appin, with the names clearly legible in fading brown ink. Their war-slogan was "Creag-an-Sgairbh" ("The Cormorant's Rock") and the Gaelic name of the clan is **Clann Stiubhart.**

Even when the '45 was over the Stewarts still suffered because when Colin Roy Campbell of Glen Ure -known as the Red Fox - was on his way to evict the Appin Stewarts from their forfeited lands he was shot off his horse and killed. James Stewart of the Glens, who was related to Ardsheal, the chief, was arrested and later tried and hanged for the murder although he was innocent. An example to others was needed. A monument to him stands on a knoll at the left-hand side of the Ballachulish road bridge as one drives north from Glen Coe or from the Oban road. Robert Louis Stevenson brought this incident into his novels 'Kidnapped" and "Catriona" and the Appin murder and who really did kill the Red Fox is a recurrent mystery.

That last gallant charge of the clans in which nearly 100 of the Appin men fell...

101

The Stewarts of Atholl, too, were staunch Jacobites and had very heavy casualties at Culloden. Colonel John Roy Stewart, of the Stuarts of Kinchardine, Inverness-shire, is fondly remembered for his courage, his piping and for composing a parody on the 23rd Psalm:

"The Lord's my targe, I will be stout
With dirk and trusty blade,
Though Campbells come in flocks about,
I will not be afraid".

The senior family of Clan Stewart is in the Lowlands. The Earls of Galloway (Chiefs of the Clan) are descended from 13th century Sir John Stewart of Bonkyl, Berwickshire, whose elder brother, James, was grandfather of King Robert III. In 1623 the head of this branch was created Earl of Galloway.

Not every Stewart is descended from royalty, and other clans claim royal descent, but few would quarrel too deeply over such a claim because it is a proud line of immense significance in British and Scottish history -James VI of Scotland became James I of England at the Union of the Crowns in 1603 - and the Highland Stewarts in particular were a tough and tenacious race.

And Finally...

One of the relatively unknown heroes of the 1745 Jacobite Rising was John MacNaughton, of Glen Lyon. He served Menzies of Culdares, a fervent Jacobite who gave a charger to Prince Charles Edward Stuart. John was captured with the rest of the garrison when Carlisle surrendered. He was sentenced to death but promised his freedom if he revealed the donor of the Prince's horse. Even on the scaffold, he refused saying freedom on such terms was not worth being despised by comrades for breaking a trust.

★   ★   ★   ★

Another hero of the 1745 Jacobite Rising was Ewen McCay who was captured carrying letters in French code and handed over to the Hanoverian military at Inverness. He refused to talk and was given 500 lashes by regimental drummers and given the opportunity, between each cut, to give the name of the person who had given him the letters. He was similarly lashed a second time and later died in his cell, still heroically silent.

★   ★   ★   ★

The MacBeths or Beatons were great exponents of medical skill and flourished in the West Highlands from the 14th century. Some of their medical treatises are among the earliest extant Gaelic manuscripts. They were based in Mull, Skye, Islay and the Uists.

★   ★   ★   ★

Gaelic legend abounds with tales of mermaids and mermen, both salt and freshwater varieties, and the Clan MacLaren claims a mermaid among its ancestors, from the island of Tiree, an event commemorated in the MacLaren coat of arms.

About the Author...

Rennie McOwan is a full-time writer and lecturer and has been hill-walking in Scotland for over 30 years.

He was a founder-member and the first president of "The Scotsman" newspaper mountaineering club (now the Ptarmigan Club, of Edinburgh) and is a founder-member and archivist of the Scottish Wild Land Group.

He belongs to a number of outdoor and conservation bodies including the Mountain Bothies Association, the National Trust for Scotland, the Scottish Rights of Way Society and the Scottish Wildlife Trust. He is an honorary member of the Clan Gregor Association and the Dollar Civic Trust.

His writings have appeared in the "Evening News", "The Scots Magazine", "The Scotsman" and "The Glasgow Herald" as well as outdoor magazines and publications in the United States.

He is a member of literary societies and a keen historian and is particularly interested in the Highlands, the Clans of old, and modern land use, and has taken part in broadcasts on outdoor topics.

For the past five years he has been guiding American walking groups in Scotland and has organised coach expeditions to outdoor and historic sites, to stately homes and to islands, and has written and delivered en-route commentaries.

He lives in Stirling, is married with four children, and his wife, Agnes is a teacher with Central Region's mobile school project to the travelling people, the tinkers.

His publications include:

Books:

"Light on Dumyat", a children's novel published by the Saint Andrew Press, of Edinburgh, and chosen by Central Region for the primary schools conference at the University of Stirling.
"Walks in the Trossachs and the Rob Roy Country". Saint Andrew Press.

Booklets:

"Tales of Stirling Castle and the Battle of Bannockburn", Lang Syne Publishing.
"Tales of Ben and Glen" (Ben Nevis), Lang Syne Publishing.
"The Man Who Bought Mountains", the story of the National Trust for Scotland's mountaineering benefactor, Percy Unna.

Contributor to:

"Walking in Scotland", Spur Books, chapters on the Southern Highlands and on the Ochils.
"Sunday Post Walks For The Family", seven routes.
"Poetry of the Scottish Hills", an anthology published by Aberdeen University Press, five poems.

Slides Lectures

Rennie McOwan gives slides-talks to groups and organisations.
They include:
(a) "A Fortnight On St. Kilda".
(b) "The Case For Wilderness", the story of Percy Unna, the National Trust for Scotland's mountaineering benefactor.
(c) "In The Hills With Colkitto and Montrose".
(d) "The Green Hills" (the Ochils).
(e) "The Witches Of The Ochils".
(f) "Sunshine and Snow", an introduction to rambling and hill-walking, particularly aimed at youth groups and beginners.